BONDS

A concise guide for investors

MOORAD CHOUDHRY

Foreword by Robert Cole

© Moorad Choudhry 2006

First published 2006 by
PALGRAVE MACMILLAN
Houndmills, Basingstoke, Hampshire RG21 6XS and
175 Fifth Avenue, New York, N.Y. 10010
Companies and representatives throughout the world

PALGRAVE MACMILLAN is the global academic imprint of the Palgrave Macmillan division of St. Martin's Press, LLC and of Palgrave Macmillan Ltd. Macmillan® is a registered trademark in the United States, United Kingdom and other countries. Palgrave is a registered trademark in the European Union and other countries.

ISBN-13: 978–0–230–00649–2
ISBN-10: 0–230–00649–3

This book is printed on paper suitable for recycling and made from fully managed and sustained forest sources.

A catalogue record for this book is available from the British Library.

10   9   8   7   6   5   4   3   2   1
15 14 13 12 11 10 09 08 07 06

Printed and bound in China

For the Raynes Park footy boys...
A Solid Bond In Your Heart

ABOUT THE AUTHOR

Moorad Choudhry is Head of Treasury at KBC Financial Products in London. He was previously a vice-president in structured finance services with JPMorgan Chase Bank in London. Prior to that he worked as a gilt-edged market maker and treasury trader with ABN Amro Hoare Govett Sterling Bonds Limited, and as a sterling proprietary trader within the Treasury division at Hambros Bank Limited.

Dr Choudhry is a Visiting Professor at the Department of Economics, London Metropolitan University, a Visiting Fellow at the ICMA Centre, University of Reading, and a Senior Fellow at the Centre for Mathematical Trading and Finance, Cass Business School. He was educated at Claremont Fan Court School in Surrey, the University of Westminster, the University of Reading, Henley Management College and Birkbeck, University of London. He has published widely in the field of debt capital markets and derivatives, including *The Bond and Money Markets: Strategy, Trading, Analysis* (Butterworth Heinemann 2001), *Capital Market Instruments: Analysis and Valuation* (FT Prentice Hall 2001), *Analysing and Interpreting the Yield Curve* (John Wiley 2004), *Structured Credit Products: Credit Derivatives and Synthetic Securitisation* (John Wiley 2004) and numerous articles in academic and trade journals.

CONTENTS

Contents

FIGURES

TABLES

Most people know about shares or equity, but for some reason there is a blind spot in the mind's eye of many private investors when it comes to bonds. Bonds are every bit as important as shares. They may be more important.

Bonds play a crucial part in any investment strategy. There is no such thing as a cast-iron guarantee but bonds give investors greater protection from capital loss than shares, and a greater certainty of receiving regular income. Buy a bond issued by the US or UK government and there is virtually no chance you will lose your money. There is every likelihood you will receive regular interest payments.

Investment markets are, almost by definition, uncertain. But if you spread savings across the four key investment asset classes you buy insurance that you will reap adequate rewards however things turn out.

The four asset classes are cash, bonds, property and shares. Cash is lowest risk and shares are highest risk. Cash also brings the least exciting prospect of reward, and shares are the opposite. But just as few investors would wisely consider buying shares without owning a house, it is also sensible that bonds take up a rightful place in any portfolio. Bond markets also provide key information to anyone trading any of the other asset classes, just as the experiences learned dealing in other assets are relevant to bondholders.

It may be useful to think of the process of investment as like driving a car and the four asset classes as the four wheels. It is only when all four wheels are working properly that the car can travel at speed in relative safety.

It is odd that private investors have a tendency to ignore bonds. It is not a problem that the average corporate investor suffers from. Moreover, as individuals grow older they should take more notice of bonds since one's exposure to risk should decline with age. As the whole population ages the bond market is also likely to play an increasingly influential role in the overall financial scene.

Professional and institutional investors do not ignore bonds. Professionals are not always right but in this instance they behave in a way that is sound. Since private and institutional investors, amateur and professional, inhabit the same environment there is no reason why they their basic patterns of behaviour should differ.

If bonds are every bit as important as shares you may ask why is there not more said about them on radio programmes and written about them in the newspapers. It is the job of journalists, however, to relate surprising and exciting items of information, and bonds are rarely surprising or exciting. Indeed bonds are often boring. But the dullness of bonds does not undermine their importance – it enhances it.

There is an Alice in Wonderland quality about a lot of the language used across the City of London, and the jargon used in relation to bonds can also appear confusing and nonsensical. But familiarity with jargon, and an understanding of the historical connections, can help explain important points of principle and practice.

Take 'gilt' for example. To the uninitiated it is a word that could have been left here by visitors from Mars. But if the word 'gilt' is put in the context of its history it quickly becomes possible to improve levels of comprehension. Understand that 'gilt' is short for 'gilt-edged security' and that 'security' is another word for bond and you will have got over the first hurdle. Appreciate that 'gilts' are bonds issued by the UK government, and that as a sign of the issuer's first-rate reliability the bond certificates used to be edged with gold leaf, and it should become clear how 'gilts' came by their name. The term 'gilt' still brings the connotation 'safety', and there lies the modern-day relevance of the older association.

Talk to a person untrained in the ways of the City or Wall Street about 'a long bond' and he or she would be forgiven for being baffled. Explain that a long bond is only a 'bond' which is set to exist for a 'long' time, however, and scales may begin to fall from eyes with remarkable speed. Talk about a 'coupon' and the uninitiated may be similarly puzzled. But explain that a coupon used to be attached to paper bond certificates, and that investors detached them at preset dates in order to qualify for interest payments, and it may become easier to understand why 'coupon' has become synonymous with the 'interest' or the 'dividend' paid on a bond.

It might be said that shares are simpler to understand than bonds, but that is a mistake. It is easier to be simplistic about shares but the reality is that shares are hugely more complicated that bonds. The simplistic analysis of shares is to say that if a company does well its shares will rise and if it does badly its shares will fall. There is truth in this, but there is a much more bewildering array of factors lying behind share price movements than bond price changes.

The essential tenets of bond investing are outlined in a clear and concise fashion in this book. Moorad Choudhry, founder and senior partner of

YieldCurve.com, has experience of the bond market that is both wide and deep. As a trader of bonds he also has an understanding of the market gleaned at first hand.

To date Moorad has written and lectured largely to a professional audience, but in this volume he uses his thorough technical knowledge to distil the key and critical aspects of the subject. *Bonds: A concise guide for investors* is a comprehensive yet comprehensible introduction to bonds. It is of value to any novice investor, and to any active investor who has unwisely skirted around the bond market to date.

Robert Cole
Editor, Tempus investment column
The Times

BONDS: THE ESSENTIAL INVESTMENT

Fixed income instruments or bonds are investment products. In this respect they are similar to bank savings accounts and equity (called shares in the UK and common stock in the USA). Virtually everybody has a savings account, and many private investors buy shares in companies. For some reason, though, they seem to shy away from bonds. This is most unfortunate, because for many investors bonds would be much more appropriate than shares, given their individual private circumstances. The general public and many small investors appear not to rate the value and importance of bonds as highly as shares. To some extent, I suspect this reflects the following beliefs:

- The bond market is not as transparent as the equity market.
- Bonds themselves are not as accessible as shares, in terms of both understanding them and actually investing in them.
- The bond market is steeped in arcane practice and technical jargon.
- There is a high level of mathematical analysis associated with bonds.

But it's all relative. Lets tackle each of these objections in turn.

Lack of transparency

The television and news media concentrate on shares, talking about individual company share prices and reporting on stock market indices like the FTSE 100 or the Dow Jones regularly each day. This makes shares seem transparent. But it's easy to check bond prices as well: just look in the *Financial Times* for gilts for example, or a website like www.gilt.co.uk. It's simply a question of knowing where to look. And the media does us all a disservice by not reporting to such extent on bonds, given the importance of the bond market in the global economy.

Lack of accessibility

Shares are easy, right? They represent an ownership in the company, and if the company is doing well, then the share price will go up and you will be doing all right. But bonds can be viewed in the same way, as loans: they represent an interest in the company, and if the company is doing well, guess what, the bond price may go up (it depends on what interest rates are doing generally). A share of a loan to the company can be much safer than a share in ownership, and there is also a fixed dividend payable, which you don't receive with many shares. What about actually investing in them? Again, you can use the same stockbroker, share shop, telephone broker or internet broker to buy and sell most bonds as you do to buy or sell shares.

Technical jargon

The equity market has its own technical terms, p/e ratio, dividend cover, and so on. Investors don't seem to have trouble with these. Certainly bond market analysis can be quite complicated, but if we describe the essential elements in the right way, it is not at all difficult to get to grips with bonds, as we shall see shortly.

High level of mathematics

OK, I'll hold up my hand here and admit to this one. Yes, to fully under-stand bonds as an analyst, investment bank strategist or university academic, you will need to be comfortable using a very high level of mathematical analysis. But don't put the book down yet, because private investors don't require this level of understanding in order to invest prof-itably in bonds. Let me put it this way. Under a certain set of assump-tions, the price of a zero-coupon bond that is free of default risk (see! I'm already exposed as someone who can't help but resort to arcane jargon. OK, but just for now – we won't need to talk like this again in the book) is given by

$$P(t,T) = \exp\left(-\int_t^T r(s)ds\right)$$

What this says is that the price of the bond is a function of the instanta-neous short-term interest rate $r(s)$, integrated over the period from now (t) to the maturity date of the bond (T).

Phew! Do we need to know this in order to understand and invest prof-itably in bonds? Of course not – and a good thing too. A quick glance at the *Financial Times* today shows me that a UK government bond, the 5% Treasury 2008, is currently priced at £99.48 for every £100 nominal or face value of stock. If I buy £1,000 nominal of this bond today, the total consideration (including accrued interest but excluding any broker's commission[1]) will be under £1,000. I will receive 5 per cent interest on my investment each year, and then on 7 March 2008 when the bond matures I will receive £1,000 back.

This is a very good investment. Period. And I don't need to be familiar with continuous-time mathematics or stochastic calculus to know this or appreciate that it is a good investment. OK, buying this bond won't make me a millionaire, but very few things will. I also know that there is absolutely no chance of the value of my investment dropping in value below the sum I paid for the bond, unless Her Majesty's Treasury goes bust. This is most unlikely, to put it mildly.

Come again?

If I buy this bond, there is no chance of the cash value of my investment dropping to below what it was when I bought it. How many equities can I say that about with absolute certainty?

THE EASY INVESTMENT

So although it is fun to delve into the intricacies of bond analysis, not only is it not necessarily to everyone's taste, it is also not required. Think of it as similar to learning to play football: practically anyone can pick up the basics of the sport and get involved in a game, but it takes a bit more effort to be selected to play in the Premiership. Just as it is not necessary to be able to pass a ball with the skill and accuracy of Steven Gerrard or David Beckham in order to enjoy a game of football, likewise we can quite comfortably understand bonds, and invest in them, without knowing about the mathematics of pricing them.[2]

In his fantastic book *A Brief History of Time*, Professor Stephen Hawking suggests that for each mathematical formula an author inserts in a book, the readership is cut by half. On this criterion, my earlier book, *Advanced Fixed Income Analytics*, would have precisely one reader! So for this book then, we will cut down mathematics to the barest minimum – just the absolute essentials needed to emphasise an illustration. In any case, as we shall see in the next few chapters, it is not necessary to be au fait with the maths of bond analysis in order to invest in them and make decent returns. Far from it, we just need the essentials, which demands no more technical skill than is associated with equities. And people seem to invest in them without qualm, so they should have no problem with bonds.

LAYOUT OF THE BOOK

This book is organised into just seven chapters. They are aimed at introducing bonds to sufficient depth so that anyone, not just market professionals, will feel comfortable about buying and holding them. The chapters cover an introduction to bonds as instruments, their importance as an integral part of the global economy, and the practical risks and rewards of holding them. There is also a detailed look at UK gilts, plus coverage of other government bonds, corporate bonds and credit ratings. We conclude with a look at relative value trading as practised in the professional market, based on the author's experience in the gilt market.

For readers' benefit we also list further reading, a glossary of frequently used terms and a selection of useful websites for the private investor.

YIELDCURVE.COM WEBSITE

Research on the debt capital markets may be downloaded from www.YieldCurve.com. This site also lists details of other books and articles written by YieldCurve.com associates. Presentations at conferences and universities, as well as television interviews, may be downloaded from the site.

Moorad Choudhry
Surrey, England

Notes

1 Don't be put off by terms such as nominal or accrued interest: they are very simple concepts and you will be very familiar with them, and other bond market terms, very shortly.
2 The pure joy and fantastic exhilaration one experiences when watching a Mr Beckham free kick go into the net, especially when he is playing for England, is however on a higher plane than the pleasure one obtains from deriving the bond price equation (but only slightly)...

The bond market is a proper market. Not like equities ...

> Sean Baguley, Managing Director, Fixed Interest
> Hoare Govett Securities Ltd, 1992

Stick to the fundamentals ... good things sometimes take time.

> Lou Mannheim in *Wall Street*,
> director Oliver Stone, 1987

CHAPTER 1

Getting to the starting point

It is generally the case that when one is introducing something of great intrinsic value, there is no need to employ marketing hype. One can just let the item speak for itself. Unfortunately this does not seem to apply to what is, undoubtedly, one of the most important elements of the global economy, and therefore of direct relevance to our collective prosperity and well-being: the bond markets. The bond market has a direct impact on anyone with a stake in the economy, whether as worker, homemaker, pensioner, student or investor. It's just that in most cases we aren't aware of this impact. But without a functioning bond market, really important things like hospitals, schools and oil refineries (and other vital things like airports, train stations and factories) wouldn't get built. And all of us, in the developed world and most of the developing world, depend on these important things to some extent.

Still, we would have no trouble finding anyone who did not quite see bonds in this way. Hence the need for some hype – at least to start with. As we get into the subject, we can start letting bonds speak for themselves. To begin with, though, we'll spend a little time confirming the importance of the bond market. We'll then look at why everyone who invests a portion of his or her earnings should be investing some of that in bonds.

Bond or fixed income instruments are associated with arcane technical jargon and a high level of mathematical analysis. But please don't trouble yourself with this, not because it is not important (it is), but because it is not necessary for what we are trying to achieve: an understanding and familiarity with bonds, such that we can go out and invest in them profitably. For the moment, take my word for it that bonds are straightforward and easy to understand, and proceed.

Let's get it on!

BONDS: IMPORTANT FOR YOU

Here is how I began Chapter 1 of an earlier book I wrote on bonds:

Readers will be familiar with the cursory slot on evening television news programmes, where the newscaster informs viewers where the main stock market index closed that day and where key foreign exchange rates closed at. In the United States most bulletins go one better and also tell us at what yield the Treasury long bond closed at. This is because bond prices are affected directly by economic and political events, and yield levels on certain government bonds are fundamental indicators of the economy. The yield level on the US Treasury long bond reflects the market's view on US interest rates, inflation, public sector debt and economic growth. Reporting the bond yield level reflects the importance of the bond market to a country's economy; this is as important as the level of the equity stock market, and more relevant as an indicator of the health and direction of the economy.

What's all that about? Yields? The Treasury long bond? How is that important to me? Lets keep it simple. Most people will at some stage of their lives need to borrow money, whether to buy a house, car or television set, pay for university, nursing home fees, and so on. Some people live in a permanent state of debt, rolling over payments on their credit cards. As readers know, when we borrow money we are required to pay it back with interest, this interest being charged at a quoted percentage rate. This interest rate is set in the bond market. So movements in the bond market directly affect our weekly cash flow. It is much more relevant for you and me, as private individuals, to know where the bond market is trading at, and hence where interest rate levels are at, then it is for us to know where the FTSE 100 or any other stock market index closed at.

A simple product

The first lesson to learn is that bonds are very simple to understand. You do not need any higher level of numeracy to understand the bond market than you do to understand the equity market, and in fact intuitively bonds are easier to grasp than equities. They are as simple as a bank savings account. You don't believe me?

Savings account

When you open a deposit account at a bank, the bank agrees to pay you a rate of interest on your money, and then return your initial amount plus interest to you when you close the account. In some cases the rate of interest might be fixed, and fixed-rate accounts usually run for a fixed term (so you can't take your money out before the term runs to maturity). Or the interest rate earned on the account can be variable, in which case the bank will inform you whenever the rate changes. On *instant-access* accounts, you can take all or part of your money out whenever you want.

The bank enters the amount you place in the account on the *liability* side of its balance sheet. In other words, the money is a *loan* to the bank. The bank uses this money as it does any money it borrows, while conducting its normal business.

Bond

When you buy a bond, the issuers of the bond agree to pay you a rate of interest, usually fixed but occasionally variable, as long as you hold the bond. If you buy the bond on the day it is issued, and hold it to maturity, you will get back your initial investment plus interest. If you want the money sooner, under certain assumptions, you will get back your initial investment plus interest. All bonds are instant-access, because you can sell all or part of your investment and get your money back at any time (as long as there is a buyer for the bond – but for the bonds that are most suitable for all investors, there is always a buyer).

The money you have used to buy the bond is a *loan* to the issuer of the bond. The issuer, which can be a government or a company, uses this loan as part of conducting its normal business.

See! Bonds are simpler than you thought. We all recognise the value and usefulness of savings accounts, and so once we become aware of the main features of bonds we should recognise their value as well. They serve many purposes and can be used to meet a wide range of investment objectives. For just about no type of investor could one categorically say that bonds had no useful value.

I have deliberately kept this simple to make a point, and not mentioned valuation, credit risk, fluctuating interest rates and a myriad other things. We can tackle these later.

When you consider investing in bonds, you should undertake analysis to determine the following:

- What rate of return do you require, or need, on your investment?
- What is the value to you now of a package of cash flows that you will receive over regular intervals over the next, say, three or five years?
- What chance is there that the country or company whose bond you are buying will go bankrupt during the time you hold the bond?

■ Where do you think inflation and the level of interest rates will be going in the next few years?

These are reasonably straightforward questions, and we can answer them in straightforward fashion. Now that the dot.com crash has made more people wary of shares (which was the one good thing to come out of that whole sorry fiasco), and made them look at alternative investments, it is important to be able to discuss bonds in clear, simple terms.

Interest rates

We are all familiar with interest rates. In the UK if you are still using certain bank credit cards, you may be paying around 15 per cent interest on any balances carried forward from month to month. If you are using a store credit card, you may be paying an even higher rate, which is quite monstrous. You may have a mortgage and be paying anything between 4 per cent and 7 per cent, depending on its type. So far then, we have identified a credit card rate and a mortgage rate.

There are many types of interest rate. All rates are based around the key government benchmark interest rate. For short-term liabilities, this might be the central bank *base rate* or *repo rate*, while for longer-dated liabilities the key interest rate is the government bond yield. We shall look at this shortly.

The bond markets are all about interest rates. Table 1.1 shows the different types of interest rate prevailing in September 2004 in the sterling market.[1] It helps us to place interest rates in context.

TABLE 1.1 Comparison of different sterling interest rates, 21 September 2004	
Bank of England base rate	4.75%
Building society ordinary account 'passbook' rate	1.55%
Building society notice account rate	3.70%
Building society two-year fixed term rate	5.40%
Three-month Treasury bill	4.79%
One-year government bond	4.66%
Five-year government bond	4.73%
Ten-year government bond	4.89%

A big market

Bonds have an esoteric, even scary, image with private investors. But they are loved by the heavyweight (and not so heavyweight) institutional investors. Fund managers, pension funds, insurance companies, hedge funds, local authority treasuries, corporates, banks and building societies all hold large quantities of bonds. Private investors should be happy to be in their company. And even if you don't hold any bonds yourself, there is a good chance that a chunk of your pension will be invested in bonds.

The bond market is very big. Table 1.2 shows the size of the just the government bond markets (bonds issued by governments) in selected countries. When you add in the corporate bond markets, the total size comes to over double the amount shown – much bigger than the global equity market.

Relevant for equity investors

Bonds are important to everyone. The state of the bond markets, and any economic signals they send out, are of relevance to all investors, even those

TABLE 1.2 Size of major government bond markets, December 2004	
Country	**Nominal value ($ billion)**
United States	6,490
Japan	2,991
Germany	1,536
France	623
Canada	371
United Kingdom	343
Netherlands	259
Australia	91
Denmark	78
Switzerland	41
Total	12,823
Source: IFC, Quarterly Bulletin.	

holding only equities. This is because just about all companies that issue shares have also issued bonds. A shareholder in a company will want to know the level of debt that the company has taken on, and also the terms under which this debt is treated in the market. This will assist the shareholder to make an informed evaluation of the company's equity. If for instance, you were aware that institutional investors were not interested in a particular company's bonds and were demanding a premium to hold them, that would give you some useful information on how that company is viewed in the market.

While the concept of shares is easily understood, and they exist pretty much everywhere in the same format, bonds come in a very large variety of shapes and sizes. This has helped to frighten private investors away from them, and explains why they turn more readily to shares. However, the main instruments that we talk about in this book, government bonds, usually exist in simple form and their mechanics can be grasped quite easily.

This is essentially what this book is all about: emphasising that bonds are very easy to understand, and informing readers about the key issues so that they can make an informed judgement about their investment needs. The right bonds really are *the essential investment*, possessing features that make them ideal for all investors. I also want to emphasise just how important the bond markets are and how they have an impact, in some way, on just about everybody. That is why it is worthwhile to keep an eye on them and on what interest rates they are trading at.

BONDS: IMPORTANT FOR EVERYONE

Most people work hard for their money. And yet, when deciding where to save some of it, they often delve into the stock market and make investment decisions based on very little knowledge. We all know (and I agree) that over the long term, the returns from investing in shares are better than those from any other investment type. But that is the key: *long* term. The term can be 30, 40 or 50 years. How many of us sit on an investment for that long? Different investors have different requirements, and over the short or medium term it is possible to lose virtually your entire capital in equity investments, or at least lose a fair chunk of it. A good many shares do not even pay a regular income, fixed or otherwise, to their owners.

When we put aside a portion of our cash we would hope to receive an income stream as well as a final return that has grown the value of that cash and also stayed ahead of inflation. What we do not want is something that returns less than the initial value of the investment. But during the stock market boom in the late 1990s, the level of hype generated about technology stocks resulted in many small investors getting into stocks that were patently unsuitable for them, with the result that many got badly burned when the market eventually tanked.[2] People were seduced by shares that could rise by 30 per cent or 50 per cent in one day, forgetting that an asset that can rise by that much can also fall in one day by the same amount. It becomes dangerous when we start looking for 'the quick buck', because that is when we are most likely to ignore or forget sensible precautions about risk and the level of volatility in the market.

Hence, all investors need to know about bonds. Specifically, they need to know about the specific types of bonds to consider whenever they need an investment that lacks much of the risk of the equity market, provides a steady income stream, and will outperform bank savings accounts.

Most private investors and small-company investors believe that the important capital market is the one in equities, with the bond market very much viewed as a sideshow and not part of the action. Bonds are staid, certainly not sexy, and associated with complex mind-numbing mathematics.

The reality is quite different. It is the bond market that is the important one, the market that influences behaviour and sentiment in the equity market. It is not the bonds themselves: in many cases they are issued by the same companies and entities that issue shares. Rather, it is the level of interest rates set in the bond markets that is the key indicator for the economy as a whole. So equity market participants take their cue from here. An understanding and appreciation of the bond markets will therefore also enable investors to better understand the equity market.

As I mentioned earlier, interest rates are set in the bond market. All the interest rate levels that we encounter in our daily lives – charged on bank loans, car loans and credit cards, and earned on savings accounts and money market funds – are linked to the rates set in the bond market. Let's look at a couple of examples.

In the UK, traditionally the interest rates on residential mortgages have been variable, based on with changes in the bank base rate. In recent years a greater number of homebuyers have been taking out fixed-rate mortgages, as these have been made available by the lenders. Generally fixed-rate mortgages are only offered for up to five years, after which the loan will be switched to a variable (floating) rate or the borrower must refinance. In the USA fixed-rate mortgages are more common. Where does the mortgage rate come from?

All interest rates are linked to their domestic government bond market. For our first lesson, let's illustrate this. In the UK, as in the USA and elsewhere, mortgage rates are very closely correlated with the yield on government bonds. Figure 1.1 shows the yield on five-year and two-year benchmark gilts since 1992, as well as a composite variable mortgage rate.[3] We see that the mortgage rate moves very tightly with the government yield. We could have illustrated this using the mortgage rate and the bank base rate, set by the Bank of England, but that wouldn't have made the point quite so well. The close correlation demonstrates our perception that interest rates are set in the bond market. We can conclude that it is important to keep an eye on yield levels in the bond market, both for general awareness and also for any insight into where rates might be heading. If we plotted the equivalent rates for the US market, we would observe the same result.

All interest rates, whether set in wholesale or retail markets, are linked to what is known as the *benchmark* rate. This is the yield applicable at any time to the benchmark government bond. There are benchmark bonds for the most popular maturities, such as two-year bonds, five-year bonds and ten-year bonds. The benchmark serves as the reference interest rate for all other interest rates of similar maturity.

So we see now that the bond market influences our lives in a very intimate way: it affects the level of cash in our pockets.

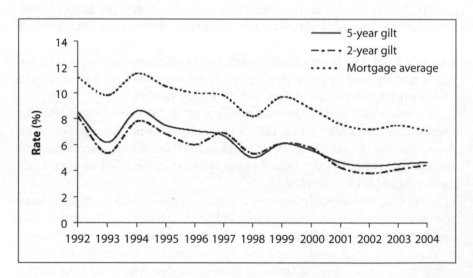

Figure 1.1 UK variable mortgage rate
and benchmark gilt rates from 1992

Source: Bloomberg, HBOS plc, Nationwide, author notes

Bonds and the global economy

At an individual level, most of us are familiar with what is required of us if we wish to raise capital. We might need capital in order to buy a house or a car, or fund further education. Or we might need finance in the form of a hire-purchase agreement. Whatever our requirement, we may need to show:

- evidence of future earnings receipts, to service the interest on the loan
- security in the form of *collateral* for the loan
- other evidence of independent wealth, or a guarantor for the loan.

Just think of the difficulty we would experience if we did not have access to credit. We would have to resort to other measures, such as selling off existing assets or going to a 'loan shark'.[4] Or we would simply have to make do without whatever goods or services we needed. It is the same for governments and companies. When they embark on a large project, they raise the funds needed in the bond market. Just think of the difficulty if they couldn't access credit! Society would not have developed as it has today, and the continuing requirements of our community would not be met.

Here is a random sample of projects that were only possible because the funding for them was available in the debt capital markets:

- the 'Marshall plan', the name given to a series of fund transfers made by the US government to continental European countries to help finance their reconstruction after the Second World War
- the creation of the National Health Service
- the construction of the railways that cross the USA
- the privatisation of former state-owned industries across Europe
- the creation and development of the petroleum industry
- the eradication of smallpox by the World Health Organization
- cheaper airfares in the airline industry as a result of private airlines entering the market
- any number of bridges, motorways, and other development infrastructure projects.

The importance of the bond markets to the well-being of the world cannot be overstated, it would seem.

If you happen to work on Wall Street or in the City, or in any financial centre in the world, the next time someone remarks that it isn't a 'real job', but just an overpaid, overblown clerical position that involves shuffling money around, you can smile to yourself because you know better![5]

Let's get back to being serious. On any given day, governments, local authorities and companies raise a large amount of cash to fund their daily activities as well as their long-term projects. In the US market alone, $3.2 trillion was raised in 2001. This is a considerable sum.

We use the term *issue* when we say that an entity has borrowed money. And we can get an insight into the economy from following the market for new issuance; this is because there is a gap from when the money is raised to when it is actually spent and finds its way into the economy.[6] So if the level of issuance is rising, we can safely conclude that the economy is set to expand. The reverse would indicate a slowing-down of the economy. This is a good indicator, containing more substance than an equity index level. But where can you obtain information on bond issues? Isn't this too technical for the layperson? Not at all – newspapers like the *Financial Times* contain this information, and the *Economist* frequently reports on capital markets activity.

This is just an example of how the bond markets have an impact on all of us, and how some sense can be made of it.

BONDS AND EQUITIES: SHOWING THE VALUE IN BONDS

We all know that equities outperform bonds 'in the long term'. That is what they *should* do, because they carry greater risk than bonds, and so would be expected to provide greater return. Consider Table 1.3, which shows the annual average real returns from UK government bonds and shares, as well as cash, since the start of the last century. Generally shares have outperformed bonds. But once in a while, bonds outperform shares. This is a bonus for bondholders, and an unexpected one. If we look at the times when this happened, we see that it was in times of market turmoil, such as the 1930s depression. So while we might conclude that it is good always to hold part of our savings in bonds, it is definitely worthwhile during a 'bear' market.[7]

We can illustrate the value of holding mixed of an investment portfolio including bonds with a simple exercise. Table 1.4 shows the value in November 2002 of £10,000 invested eight years earlier. Portfolio 1 is a fund that tracks the FTSE-100 index, which is the main UK equity market stock index, while Portfolio 2 is a 50:50 mix of the FTSE tracker fund and the benchmark UK gilt bond. We see that Portfolio 2 compares very favourably with the all-equity portfolio, and in fact provides good safety when the equity market is not performing well.

TABLE 1.3 UK market return performance			
	Gilts (%)	Shares %	Cash %
1991–2001	9.4	11.8	4.2
1999–2000	6.1	– 8.6	3.2
1960–1979	– 2.7	1.1	– 0.9
1920–1928	13.9	18.0	10.2
1929–1933	17.4	10.5	6.1
1901–2001	1.1	5.5	0.9
Source: Barclays Capital.			

The year 2002 was just such a year when equities did not perform well. Figure 1.2 shows an extract from *The Times* newspaper in the UK. It shows that while the main equity index was down more than 24 per cent in the year, government bonds (gilts) were up more than 4 per cent.

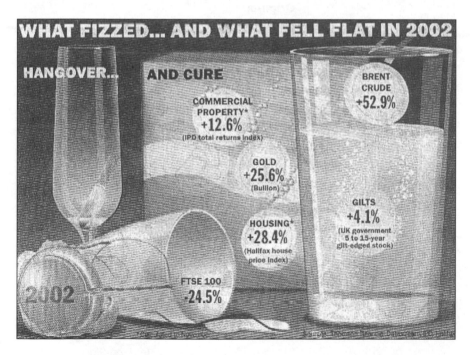

Figure 1.2 Extract from *The Times*, 1 January 2003
© News International. Reproduced with permission.

TABLE 1.4 Performance comparison of equity tracker portfolio and equity-bond portfolio					

Portfolio 1:   Equity portfolio

Portfolio 2:   50% equity + 50% UK gilt benchmark portfolio

Value today of £10,000 invested in:

Date	FTSE 100	Port 1	Equity	Bond	Port 2
Nov-02	4169	10,000	5,000	5,000.00	10,000.00
Nov-01	5203	8,013	4,006	4,945.10	8,951.44
Nov-00	6142	6,788	3,394	5,033.43	8,427.28
Nov-99	6597	6,320	3,160	5,095.24	8,255.01
Nov-98	5743	7,259	3,630	4,803.12	8,432.75
Nov-97	4831	8,630	4,315	5,237.03	9,551.87
Nov-96	4058	10,274	5,137	5,480.50	10,617.27
Nov-95	3664	11,378	5,689	5,630.41	11,319.55
Nov-94	3081	13,531	6,766	5,978.56	12,744.22

	UKT 6T 04	Price	Original invest- ment value	Nominal	Value today
Nov-02		105.39	£5,978	4,744.28	5,000.00
Nov-01		106.56	£6,044	4,692.19	4,945.10
Nov-00		104.69	£5,938	4,776.01	5,033.43
Nov-99		103.42	£5,866	4,834.65	5,095.24
Nov-98		109.71	£6,223	4,557.47	4,803.12
Nov-97		100.62	£5,707	4,969.19	5,237.03
Nov-96		96.15	£5,453	5,200.21	5,480.50
Nov-95		93.59	£5,308	5,342.45	5,630.41
Nov-94		88.14	£5,000	**5,672.79**	5,978.56

Sett date and value date is 26 Nov (0 days accrued)

Coupon date is 26 May and 26 Nov

Coupon received is £382.86 per year

Price at 20 December 2002 is 105.36

But it isn't a competition, or a matter of one over the other. The aim of this book is not to rubbish equities (however much we might want to!), but to show that all investors should consider bonds as *part* of their portfolio. Because they are on the whole safer than equities, investors should ideally be holding bonds before they consider equities. That's just common sense: if your life savings amounted to £500, you wouldn't place it all in the Japanese warrant market. You would be advised to place it in a bank account. As you saved more money, you might want to place some of it in other investments, from government bonds and then on to equities. It's a gradation of risk. This is the sensible approach. So it is worth your while, irrespective of whether you hold bonds or intend to, to be aware of their main characteristics and how they compare with equities.

We can do this in bullet point form:

- Shares represent ownership in a company. Shareholders are owners of the company and have voting rights at the annual general meeting. They receive a dividend only after all other claims on the company have been met. Bonds represent a company's debt, and bondholders rank above shareholders in the event of a winding-up of the company.
- Bonds (generally) have a fixed maturity date, when the face value of the bond is paid back. They (generally) pay a fixed rate of interest or *coupon*. The dividend on a share is not guaranteed.
- The tax treatment of bonds sometimes differs from that of shares. For instance, UK gilts are not subject to capital gains tax in the way that shares are.

Shares are generally recommended as being for the long term, and for those investors who do not require a regular income on their investments. The main return for shareholders is the capital gain that results when the share price rises. Bonds however can combine income with an element of capital gain, and are less price volatile than shares, so they are suitable even for those who might be commonly expected to be share investors. We examine this in subsequent chapters.

A SUMMARY TO FINISH THE FIRST CHAPTER

The foregoing has served, I hope, to illustrate the importance of the bond markets, and how they have an impact on most of us. The influence of the market is felt in a number of activities that we engage in, mainly connected with borrowing money.

So if you are a private investor or small investor who already holds bonds, this book should help you understand better your investments. If you do not hold bonds, hopefully this book will demonstrate why they should be an important part of your savings. However one does not need to be a fixed income investor to benefit from a better understanding of bonds and the bond market. The impact of bonds is so great, and the behaviour of the market so influential, that even equity investors will gain a better appreciation of the economic fundamentals that govern the movement of share prices.

To conclude this first chapter, let's summarise some key points:

- Bonds can be very good investments for most people. Bonds issued by certain governments such as gilts are safer than a bank or building society savings account, while offering a better return.
- Bonds exhibit lower price volatility than shares. This is a good thing in times of depressed stock markets, such as that experienced after the technology stocks downturn, or after the events of September 2001.
- Buying bonds means one is lending money to the issuer. In return for this, the bondholder receives a regular coupon payment, which is the interest payable by the bond issuer. On maturity of the bond, the bondholder receives the face value of the bond.
- The regular payment feature means that bonds are ideal investments for most people, and probably more ideal the older an investor is. A commonly heard suggestion is that the percentage of our savings held in bonds should be equal to our age.[8]
- There is a large variety of bonds in issue, some of them very safe and easy to understand, such as gilts, and some of them distinctly unsafe and not easy to understand, such as high-yield bonds or collateralised debt obligations.

Now that we understand all this, it's time to delve deeper into bonds.

Notes

1 That means for sterling as a currency. In other words, the rates prevailing in the UK, which is the country that issues sterling cash.
2 The occasional use of jargon whose meaning is self-evident will be tolerated in this book. We could use the technical term, a market *correction*, which is what we say when we mean that the level of the market is unjustifiably high and is due for a fall at some point.
3 'Correlate' is to show a mutual, complementary or reciprocal relationship. There is no one 'mortgage rate', so we have taken the average from the quoted variable rate as set by

Halifax Building Society (subsequently Halifax plc and then HBOS plc), Nationwide Building Society, HSBC, Woolwich plc and Abbey National plc. This sample has not really been picked quite in keeping with the niceties of econometrics: the first two institutions publish readily available data, and the last three have all advanced mortgages at one time or another to the author!

4   We do not use this term in a judgmental way. An individual who makes credit available to people in the community, whether at reasonable or exorbitant interest rates, or who uses unscrupulous methods to recover the loans (s)he has made, is nevertheless meeting a demand in the market. We may think that such an individual is odious or loathsome, but if there were no demand for funds such a person would not exist. Perhaps one of the less-highlighted achievements of the bond markets is that they made credit available to a wider and larger group of people, of diverse backgrounds, such that the requirement for unregulated money lenders decreased.

5   Not that anyone has ever said this to the author. Well, not quite – not recently – not this week anyway....

6   This is because it is not spent all in one go! Governments will need to disburse the funds to the relevant departments, who will channel it further; companies will need to complete planning for their projects and then actually implement the project itself. This all takes time.

7   Jargon watch: 'real' return is return adjusted for inflation: that is, we take out the impact of inflation. A 'bear' market is a market that is moving downwards, as opposed to a 'bull' market which is moving upwards. Since we want the value of our investments to go up, a bull market is always preferable, unless we are 'short' the market. But let's forget that for the moment.

8   This is not a bad suggestion. However at the time of writing, the author held more than 39 per cent of his savings in bonds, so he overstepped this guideline!

CHAPTER 2

Bond basics

Bond and shares form part of the *capital markets*. Shares are *equity capital* while bonds are *debt capital*. So bonds are a form of debt, much as a bank loan is a form of debt. Unlike bank loans, however, bonds can be *traded* in a market. A bond is a debt capital market instrument issued by a borrower, who is then required to repay to the lender/investor the amount borrowed plus interest, over a specified period of time. Bonds are also known as *fixed income* instruments, or *fixed interest* instruments in the sterling markets. Usually bonds are considered to be those debt securities with terms to maturity of over one year. Debt issued with a maturity of less than one year is considered to be *money market* debt. There are many different types of bonds that can be issued. The most common bond is the *conventional* (or *plain vanilla* or *bullet*) bond. This is a bond paying regular (annual or semi-annual) interest at a fixed rate over a fixed period to maturity or redemption, with the return of *principal* (the par or nominal value of the bond) on the maturity date. All other bonds are variations on this.

The different types of bond in the market reflect the different types of issuers and their requirements. Some bonds are safer investments than others. The advantage of bonds to an investor is that they represent a fixed source of current income, with an assurance of repayment of the loan on maturity. Bonds issued by developed country governments are deemed to be guaranteed investments, in that the final repayment is virtually certain. In the event of default of the issuing entity, bondholders rank above shareholders for compensation payments. There is lower risk associated with bonds than with shares as an investment, and therefore almost invariably a lower return over the long term.

We can now look in more detail at some important features of bonds.

DESCRIPTION

We have said that a bond is a debt instrument, usually paying a fixed rate of interest over a fixed period of time. It is a collection of cash flows, as

Bonds

illustrated in Figure 2.1. This shows an hypothetical example, where the bond is a six-year issue that pays fixed interest payments of C per cent of the *nominal* value on an annual basis. In the sixth year there is a final interest payment and the loan proceeds represented by the bond are also paid back, known as the maturity proceeds. The amount raised by the bond issuer is dependent on the price of the bond at issue, usually *par* or 100 per cent of face value, which we have labelled here as the issue proceeds.

The upward-facing arrow represents the cash flow paid, and the downward-facing arrows are the cash flows received by the bond investor. The cash flow diagram for a six-year bond that had a 5 per cent fixed interest rate, known as a 5 per cent *coupon*, would show interest payments of £5 per every £100 of bonds, with a final payment of £105 in the sixth year, representing the last coupon payment and the redemption payment. Again, the amount of funds raised per £100 of bonds depends on the price of the bond on the day it is first issued, and we shall look further into this later. If our example bond paid its coupon on a semi-annual basis, the cash flows would be £2.50 every six months until the final redemption payment of £102.50.

Gilts and US government bonds, known as Treasuries, pay coupon every six months. Other bonds pay annual coupon or quarterly coupon.

Let us examine some of the key features of bonds.

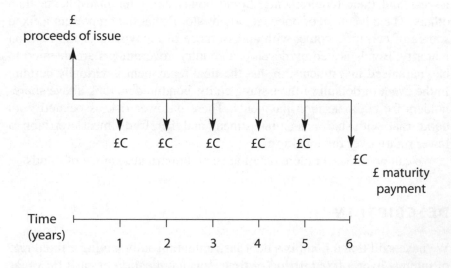

Figure 2.1 Cash flows associated with a six-year annual coupon bond

Type of issuer

The primary distinguishing feature of a bond is its issuer. The nature of the issuer will affect the way the bond is viewed in the market. There are four issuers of bonds: sovereign governments and their agencies, local government authorities, supranational bodies such as the World Bank, and corporations. Within the corporate bond market there is a wide range of issuers, each with differing abilities to satisfy their contractual obligations to investors. The largest bond markets are those of sovereign borrowers, the government bond markets.

Term to maturity

The *term to maturity* of a bond is the number of years after which the issuer will repay the obligation. The *maturity* of a bond refers to the date that the debt will cease to exist, at which time the issuer will redeem the bond by paying back to bondholders the *principal* or face value. The term to maturity is an important consideration in the make-up of a bond. It indicates the time period over which the bondholder can expect to receive the coupon payments and the number of years before the principal will be paid in full. The bond's *yield* also depends on the term to maturity. Finally, the price of a bond will fluctuate over its life as yields in the market change and as it approaches maturity. As we shall discover later, the *volatility* of a bond's price is dependent on its maturity; assuming other factors remain constant, the longer a bond's maturity the greater the price volatility resulting from a change in market yields.

Principal and coupon rate

The *principal* of a bond is the amount that the issuer agrees to repay the bondholder on the maturity date. This amount is also referred to as the *redemption value, maturity value, par value* or *face amount*, or simply *par*. The *coupon rate* or *nominal rate* is the interest rate that the issuer agrees to pay each year. The annual amount of the interest payment made is called the *coupon*. The coupon rate multiplied by the principal of the bond provides the cash amount of the coupon. For example a bond with a 7 per cent coupon rate and a principal of £1,000,000 will pay annual interest of £70,000. In the UK, USA and Japan the usual practice is for the issuer to pay the coupon in two semi-annual installments. For bonds issued in European markets and the Eurobond market, coupon payments are made annually. On occasion one will encounter bonds that pay interest on a quarterly basis. All bonds make periodic interest payments except for *zero-coupon bonds*. These bonds allow a holder to realise interest by being sold substantially below their principal value. The bonds are redeemed at par, with the interest amount then being the difference between the principal value and the price at which the bond was sold. We explore zero-coupon bonds in greater detail later.

Currency

Bonds can be issued in virtually any currency. The largest volume of bonds in the global markets is denominated in US dollars; other major bond markets are denominated in euros, sterling and Japanese yen. There are also liquid markets in Australian, New Zealand and Canadian dollars, Swiss francs and other major currencies.

BOND ISSUERS

The core of any domestic capital market is the government bond market, which also forms the benchmark for all other borrowing. Figure 2.2 illustrates UK gilt price and yield quotes as listed in the *Financial Times* for 25 January 2006.

From Figure 2.2 we can see that the 5% 2012 stock closing price from the day before was 104.62, which means £104.62 of par value. (Remember that par is the lump sum paid at maturity). This price represents a *gross redemption yield* of 4.14 per cent.[1] If we pay £104.62 per £100 of stock today, we shall receive £100 per £100 of stock on maturity. At first sight this appears to imply we shall lose money. However we also receive coupon payments every six months, which for this bond is £2.50 per £100 nominal of stock.

Also from Figure 2.2 we see the change in price from the day before for each gilt, and in the case of the 5% 2012 the price was £0.03 higher than the previous day's closing price.

Government agencies also issue bonds. Such bonds are virtually as secure as government bonds. In the USA, agencies include the Federal National Mortgage Association. Local authorities issue bonds as part of financing for roads, schools, hospitals and other capital projects.

Corporate borrowers issue bonds both to raise finance for major projects and to cover ongoing and operational expenses. Corporate finance is a mixture of debt and equity, and a specific capital project will often be financed as a mixture of both.

UK GILTS - cash market

www.ft.com/gilts

Jan 24	Price £	Red Yield	Change in Yield				52 week		Amnt £m
			Day	Week	Month	Year	High	Low	
Tr 7½pc '06	102.68xd	4.30	+.02	+.08	+.14	+.14	105.41	**102.68**	11,807
Tr 4½pc '07	100.26	4.26	+.02	+.08	+.13	+.14	100.78	99.39	11,500
Tr 5pc '08	101.49	4.25	+.03	+.09	+.03	+.08	102.49	100.44	14,221
Tr 4pc '09	99.28	4.25	+.03	+.09	+.01	+.06	99.91	96.93	16,616
Tr 4¾pc '10	102.13	4.21	+.02	+.09	−.01	+.04	103.05	99.49	9,250
Cn 9pc Ln '11	123.34	4.18	+.01	+.08	−.04	+.02	125.94	122.33	5,396
Tr 5pc '12	104.62	4.14	+.03	+.08	−.06	−	105.27	100.76	13,346
Tr 8pc '13	125.57	4.08	+.02	+.06	−.11	−.04	126.66	121.64	6,181
Tr 5pc '14	106.74	4.06	+.02	+.05	−.13	−.05	107.25	100.94	13,050
Tr 4¾pc '15	105.66	4.03	+.02	+.05	−.15	−.07	106.18	99.06	13,000
Tr 4¾pc '20	108.37	3.97	+.02	+.03	−.20	−.13	109.01	103.18	8,069
Tr 8pc '21	145.75	3.99	+.02	+.04	−.19	−.12	146.62	135.13	16,741
Tr 5pc '25	115.19	3.87	+.01	+.02	−.25	−.18	115.82	102.54	15,422
Tr 6pc '28	133.38	3.80	−	+.01	−.29	−.22	134.07	117.52	11,756
Tr 4¼pc '32	108.45	3.74	−	−	−.32	−.26	109.01	92.62	16,961
Tr 4¼pc '36	109.87	3.70	−	−.01	−.33	−.27	110.42	92.49	15,338
Tr 4¾pc '38	120.31	3.68	−	−.01	−.34	−.28	120.90	100.88	14,250
Tr 4¼pc '55	116.17	3.56	−.01	−.03	−.37	−.32	116.31	98.89	7,102
War Ln 3½pc	93.13	−	−	−	−	−	93.90	73.50	1,939

xd Ex dividend. Closing mid-prices are shown in pounds per £100 nominal of stock. Red yield: Gross redemption yield. This table shows the gilt benchmarks & the non-rump undated stocks. A longer list appears on Mondays & the full list on Saturdays, and can be found daily on ft.com/bonds&rates.   Source: Debt Management Office (DMO).

Figure 2.2 UK gilts prices page for 25 January 2006

Reprinted from the *Financial Times*. © Pearson Group. Used with permission

What bonds are not

Before proceeding with our discussion, let's consider a number of investments that are called 'bonds' in the financial media and by financial advisors, but are not the bonds that we are talking about in this book.

SAVINGS BONDS

These are marketed by banks and building societies, but they are in fact savings accounts. The difference is that they have fixed interest rates or fixed terms, unlike instant access savings accounts, and so investors cannot access their money until the term is completed.

WITH-PROFITS BONDS

These are savings plans that are usually set for ten-year terms or longer. They are offered by life assurance companies. Savers invest a lump sum or regular monthly amounts into a plan that is invested in the 'with-profits' fund of the life company, which is designed to smooth out the cyclical return patterns of the stock market. With-profit funds are overwhelmingly invested in equities.

PREMIUM BONDS

These are a glorified type of lottery, with the added advantage that investors can get their investment back at any time. Premium bonds are entered in a prize draw, with a sliding scale of prizes.

GUARANTEED INCOME BONDS

This is another product offered by life assurance companies, in which a lump sum is invested for a fixed term. The return is guaranteed during this term, and the original capital investment returned on maturity.

BABY BONDS

These are offered by life companies, and are another form of regular savings in a with-profits fund.

TYPES OF BONDS

The needs of about 95 per cent of private investors will be met by conventional bonds. But as we noted in Chapter 1, bonds come in a variety of shapes and sizes. Let's consider these here.

Conventional bonds

These are the most common type, and have a fixed coupon and fixed maturity date. They are also known as *bullet, straight* or *vanilla* bonds.

Government bonds

These are bonds issued by governments, and include the safest investments in the market, such as UK gilts, US Treasuries, German Bunds and so on.

Floating rate notes

The bond market is often referred to as the *fixed income* market, or the *fixed interest* market in the UK. Floating rate notes (FRNs) do not have a fixed coupon at all but instead link their interest payments to an external reference, such as the three-month bank lending rate. Bank interest rates will fluctuate constantly during the life of the bond, and so an FRN's cash flows are not known with certainty. Usually FRNs pay a fixed margin or *spread* over the specified reference rate; occasionally the spread is not fixed and such a bond is known as a *variable rate note*. Because FRNs pay coupons based on the three-month or six-month bank rate, they are essentially money market instruments and are treated by bank dealing desks as such.

Index-linked bonds

An index-linked bond has its coupon and redemption payment, or sometimes just one of these, linked to a specified index. When governments issue index-linked bonds the cash flows are linked to a price index such as consumer or commodity prices. Corporates have issued index-linked bonds that are connected to inflation or a stock market index.

Zero-coupon bonds

Certain bonds do not make any coupon payments at all and these are known as *zero-coupon bonds*. A zero-coupon bond or *strip* has only one cash flow, the redemption payment on maturity. If we assume that the maturity payment is say, £100, the issue price will be at a discount to par. Such bonds are also known therefore as *discounted* bonds. The difference between the price paid on issue and the redemption payment is the interest realised by the bondholder. As we shall discover when we look at strips, this has certain advantages for investors, the main one being that there are no coupon payments to be invested during the bond's life. Both governments and corporates issue zero-coupon bonds.

Corporate bonds

These are bonds issued by non-government entities, and can be conventional bonds or a variation on a theme. Corporate bonds exhibit varying degrees of credit risk, because they are not risk-free like gilts. The yield payable on a corporate bond will depend on how risky its issuer is perceived in the market.

High yield bonds

These are also known as *junk bonds*, and are issued by companies that have a *credit rating* below *investment grade*. This means that the company represents a higher risk for investors than usual, and so the yield on the bond is considerably higher than (say) government bonds or investment grade companies. They are, almost invariably, not suitable for private investors.

Eurobonds

These are also known as international securities, and are issued by governments and companies to investors around the world.[2] They are generally conventional bonds, but include a large class of bonds known as *asset-backed securities*. These are not generally suitable for private investors.

Bonds with embedded options

Some bonds include a provision that gives either the bondholder and/or the issuer an option to select early redemption of the bond. The most common type of option embedded in a bond is a *call feature*. A call provision grants the issuer the right to redeem all or part of the debt before the specified maturity date. An issuing company may wish to include such a feature as it allows it to replace an old bond issue with a lower coupon rate issue if interest rates in the market have declined. As a call feature allows the issuer to change the maturity date of a bond it is considered harmful to the bondholder's interests; therefore the market price of the bond at any time will reflect this.

A bond issue may also include a provision that allows the investor to change the maturity of the bond. This is known as a *put feature* and gives the bondholder the right to sell the bond back to the issuer at par on specified dates. The advantage to the bondholder is that if interest rates rise after the issue date, thus depressing the bond's value, the investor can realise par value by *putting* the bond back to the issuer.

A *convertible* bond is an issue giving the bondholder the right to exchange the bond for a specified amount of shares (equity) in the issuing company. This feature allows the investor to take advantage of favourable movements in the price of the issuer's shares.

Bond warrants

A bond may be issued with a warrant attached to it, which entitles the bond holder to buy more of the bond (or a different bond issued by the same borrower) under specified terms and conditions at a later date. An issuer may include a warrant in order to make the bond more attractive to investors. Warrants are often detached from their host bond and traded separately.

Asset-backed securities

These are bonds formed from pooling together a set of loans such as mortgages or car loans and issuing bonds against them. The interest payments on the original loans serve to back the interest payable on the asset-backed bond. They are not marketed to private investors and we shall not be considering these instruments in this book.

THE QUEASY STUFF: PRICE AND YIELD

In the preface I noted Professor Steven Hawking's belief that for each mathematical equation in a book, the readership is cut by half. Regrettably then, in this chapter I'm going to lose some of my readers. But I won't forget Professor Hawking's dictum: I'll keep the numbers stuff to a minimum. In fact, I'm going to prove once and for all that it is possible to understand bonds without having to get into the maths.

Financial arithmetic

I have already described bonds as a package of cash flows. That is, a bond is a contract that states that the borrower (issuer) of the funds will pay a specified rate of interest on the borrowed money for the life of the deal, and then repay the loan in full on the maturity date. In other words, a bond is a package of *future cash flows*. What would you pay now for a package of future cash flows, if you were offered one?

Essentially, you would like to pay the fair price for such a package. But what is its fair value? Actually, we are not going too far from the truth if we say that the fair price of anything is the price at which a buyer and seller can agree. However both parties need to be fully informed. For bonds, it's all concerned with *discounting* and *present value*. We wish to know the present value of a package of future cashflows.

That's what we're going to talk about now. Trust me, it's a piece of cake!

Discounting and present value

The principles of compound interest have long been used to illustrate that

£1 received today is not the same as £1 received at a point in the future. Faced with a choice between receiving £1 today or £1 in one year's time, we would pick the £1 now – because there is no uncertainty that we shall have it in our hands! However if we were offered the £1 in the future together with some interest, then we might agree to forgo the £1 now, just as long the interest rate offered was sufficient for us.

Say this rate of interest is 10 per cent per annum. Our choice would be between £1 today and £1 plus 10p – the interest on £1 for one year at 10 per cent per annum – in a year's time. But the further one goes into the future, the greater will be our requirement to be compensated for interest forgone, because of the effect of *compounding*. This is where we earn interest on our interest, provided it is added to the original investment and not spent, and it is an important concept for private investors.

In compounding we seek to find a *future value* given a *present value*, a *time period* and an *interest rate*. If £100 is invested today (at time t_0) at 10 per cent, one year later (t_1) the investor will have £100 × (1 + 0.10) = £110. If she leaves the capital and interest for another year she will have at the end of year 2 (t_2):

$$£110 \times (1 + 0.10)$$
$$= £100 \times (1 + 0.10) \times (1 + 0.10)$$
$$= £100 \times (1 + 0.10)^2$$
$$= £121.$$

The outcome of the process of compounding is the *future value* of the initial amount. Therefore we can use the following expression

$$FV = PV\,(1+r)^n \tag{2.1}$$

where

FV is the future value
PV is initial outlay or present value
r is the periodic rate of interest (expressed as decimal)
n is the number of periods for which the sum is invested.

The expression (2.1) assumes *annual compounding*. Where semi-annual or quarterly compounding takes place, the equation needs to be modified slightly. We shall receive a bit more interest, the greater the frequency of compounding.

Discounting

But what about bonds? They are a package of future cash flows. In other words, it is not the future value we want to find with them, because we already know what that is! If I want to buy a bond, I actually need to find its price today, which is the *present value* (*PV*) of a known future sum. Easy, we simply reverse the expression at (2.1), as shown:

$$PV = \frac{FV}{(1 + r)^n} \qquad\qquad (2.2)$$

where the letters *PV, r* and *n* mean the same things as before.

Example 2.1

Angela needs to have £1000 in three years time to pay for a trip round the world. She can invest at 9 per cent. How much does she need to invest now?

To solve this we require the present value of £1000 received in three years time, given that the interest rate (the discount rate) is 9 per cent. This is given by:

$$PV = \frac{1000}{(1 + 0.09)^3}$$

$$= \frac{1000}{1.295} = £772.20$$

In other words, Angela needs to invest about £773 now.

Compounding more than once a year

When interest is compounded more than once a year, the formula for calculating present values must be modified, as shown below.

$$PV = \frac{C_n}{\left(1 + \dfrac{r}{m}\right)^{mn}} \qquad\qquad (2.3)$$

where C_n is the cash flow at the end of year n, m is the number of times a year interest is compounded, and r is the rate of interest as before. Therefore the present value of £100 to be received at the end of year 3, at a rate of interest rate of 10 per cent compounded quarterly, is:

$$PV = \frac{100}{\left(1 + \dfrac{0.10}{4}\right)^{(4)(3)}}$$

$$= £74.36$$

Pricing bonds

So now we can easily determine what the price of a bond is: it is its *present value*. In other words, its price is equal to the present value of all its expected cash flows. A vanilla bond pays a fixed rate of interest (coupon) annually, semi-annually or quarterly. The *fair price* of such a bond is given by the discounted present value of all its cash flows, which we know. We obtain the present value by discounting the cash flows using a discount rate, which is in fact the bond's *gross redemption yield* or *yield to maturity* and is the rate r that appears in the expression (2.4).

$$P = \frac{C}{(1+r)} + \frac{C}{(1+r)^2} + \dots\dots + \frac{C}{(1+r)^{2T-1}} + \frac{C}{(1+r)^{2T}} + \frac{M}{(1+r)^{2T}}$$

$$= \sum_{t=1}^{2T} \frac{C}{(1+r)^t} + \frac{M}{(1+r)^{2T}} \tag{2.4}$$

where

P is the fair price of the bond
C is the annual fixed coupon payment
M is the par value of the bond (usually 100)
T is the number of complete years to maturity
r is the market-determined discount rate or required rate of return for the bond.

For a bond that pays coupons semi-annually, like gilts, the expression is modified as shown below:

$$P = \frac{C/2}{(1 + \tfrac{1}{2}r)} + \frac{C/2}{(1 + \tfrac{1}{2}r)^2} + \ldots\ldots + \frac{C/2}{(1 + \tfrac{1}{2}r)^{2T-1}} + \frac{C/2}{(1 + \tfrac{1}{2}r)^{2T}} + \frac{M}{(1 + \tfrac{1}{2}r)^{2T}}$$

$$= \sum_{t=1}^{2T} \frac{C/2}{(1 + \tfrac{1}{2}r)^t} + \frac{M}{(1 + \tfrac{1}{2}r)^{2T}} \tag{2.5}$$

Looks scary doesn't it! But trust me, it isn't!

All (2.5) is saying is that we calculate the present value of each coupon, as well as the principal payment, and add all these amounts together. The funny squiggly sign, Σ, the Greek letter sigma, just means 'add up'.

Of course, from above we see that the expression (2.4) contains two unknowns, the price and the redemption yield. I hope you remember from your O-level maths that you cannot solve two unknowns from only one equation, so you have to solve it iteratively. Do you have to be bothered with that? Not really: it's much easier to use a financial calculator such as a Hewlett Packard, or a computer program like Excel. The appendix on page 44 shows how to do it using Excel. Now that really is easy!

Clean and dirty bond prices: accrued interest

The bond price given by (2.4) is what is know as the *clean price*. When you buy a bond, you pay what is known as the *dirty price*. After a buy or sell transaction, there is a day when the buyer hands over her cash and the seller hands over the bond. This will *not* be the same day that the transaction or bargain takes place: it will be one, two, three or more days later, and is known as the s*ettlement* date.

Unless the settlement date is the same day as the coupon date, the clean price will always be different from the dirty price. This is because we need to allow for what is known as *accrued interest*.

The clean price excludes coupon interest that has accrued on the bond since the last coupon payment. All bonds accrue interest on a daily basis, so that even if a bond is held for only one day, interest will have been earned by the bondholder. The price that is actually paid for the bond in the market is the *dirty price* (or *gross price*), which is the clean price plus accrued interest. In other words the accrued interest must be added to the quoted price to get the total consideration for the bond.

Accrued interest compensates the seller of the bond for giving up all of the next coupon payment even though she will have held the bond for part of the period since the last coupon payment. The clean price for a bond will move with changes in market interest rates; assuming that this is constant in a coupon period, the clean price will be constant for this period. However the dirty price for the same bond will increase steadily from one interest payment date until the next one. On the coupon date the clean and dirty prices are the same and the accrued interest is zero. Between the coupon payment date and the next *ex dividend* date the bond is traded *cum dividend*, so that the buyer gets the next coupon payment. The seller is compensated for not receiving the next coupon payment by receiving accrued interest instead. This is positive and increases up to the next ex dividend date, at which point the dirty price falls by the present value of the amount of the coupon payment. The dirty price at this point is below the clean price, reflecting the fact that accrued interest is now negative. This is because after the ex dividend date the bond is traded 'ex-dividend': the seller not the buyer receives the next coupon and the buyer has to be compensated for not receiving the next coupon by means of a lower price for holding the bond.

Not all markets have an ex-dividend period: some trade cum dividend right up to the coupon date. Gilts do have an ex-dividend period.

In an ideal word, to calculate accrued interest we would take the number of days we had held the bond (actual days) and divide by 365. We would then multiply the bond coupon by this fraction. In other words, the formula *should* be

$$AI = C \times \frac{act}{365} \qquad\qquad (2.6)$$

where *AI* is the accrued interest.

In fact it isn't, not for a lot of bonds anyway. If you come across this formula in a book, be aware that it will give you a good approximation but not the precise value. Gilts, Treasuries and a lot of euro government bonds calculate accrued interest on what is known as an *ACT/ACT* basis, but unless we are dealing in large sums, it is not really an issue.

Example 2.2: accrued interest calculation for 7% Treasury 2002

This bond has coupon dates of 7 June and 7 December each year. Say that £100 nominal of the bond is traded for value on 27 August 1998, at a clean price of £98.25. What is accrued interest on the value date and the total consideration?

On the value date 81 days has passed since the last coupon date. Under the old system for gilts, ACT/365, the calculation was:

$$7 \times \frac{81}{365} = 1.55342$$

Under the current system of *ACT/ACT*, which came into effect for gilts in November 1998, the accrued calculation uses the actual number of days between the two coupon dates, giving us:

$$7 \times \frac{81}{183} \times 0.5 = 1.54918$$

We add this to the clean price to obtain a dirty price of £98.799 (rounded to £98.80) per £100 face value of bond. Simple!

Bond yields

There are various types of yield measure used in the market. We need only concern ourselves with two, the simple yield or *running yield* and the *redemption yield*.

Running yield

The simplest measure of the yield on a bond is the *current yield* (or *flat yield, interest yield* or *running yield*). This is defined as

$$rc = \frac{C}{P} \times 100 \tag{2.7}$$

where

rc is the current yield
C is the coupon rate
P is the clean price.

The current yield is useful as a 'rough-and-ready' interest rate calculation; it is often used to estimate the cost of or profit from a short-term holding of a bond. For example if you buy a bond, hold it for several months and then sell it, the running yield is what you would have earned during this period. It is a good approximation, and enables you to compare the return on the bond holding with a bank account or other return. Figure 2.2 (page 21) shows the running yield for each gilt as well as the redemption yield.

Example 2.3: running yield

If the clean price of a bond is £98.76 and the coupon is 6.00 per cent then the current yield is

$$rc = \frac{6.00}{98.76} \times 100$$

$$= 6.075\%$$

Yield to maturity

The *yield to maturity* (YTM) or *gross redemption yield* is the most frequently used measure of return from holding a bond. It takes into account the pattern of coupon payments, the bond's term to maturity and the capital gain (or loss) arising over the remaining life of the bond. We know the expression for it already – it is the rate r given in (2.4) earlier. This uses r to discount the bond's cash flows back to the next coupon payment and then discounts the value at that date back to date t. In other words r is the *internal rate of return* (IRR) that equates the value of the discounted cash flows on the bond to the current dirty price of the bond (if date t is the current date). The internal rate of return is the discount rate which, if applied to all of the cash flows, will solve for a number that is equal to the dirty price of the bond (its present value). If it is assumed that this rate will be unchanged for the reinvestment of all the coupon cash flows, and that the instrument will be held to maturity, the IRR can then be seen as the yield to maturity.

Note that the redemption yield as calculated by equation (2.4) is the *gross redemption yield*, the yield that results from payment of coupons without deduction of any withholding tax. The *net redemption yield* is obtained by multiplying the coupon rate by (1 – marginal tax rate). The net redemption yield is lower than the gross redemption yield.

What does the redemption yield tell us?

While redemption yield is the most commonly used measure of yield, it has one major disadvantage. The disadvantage is that implicit in its calculation is the assumption that each coupon payment as it becomes due is reinvested at the rate r. This is clearly unlikely, because of the fluctuations in interest rates over time and as the bond approaches maturity. In

practice the measure itself will not equal the actual return from holding
the bond, even if it is held to maturity. That said, the market standard is
to quote bond returns as yields to maturity, bearing the key assumptions
behind the calculation in mind, so that you can compare yields across
different bonds and investments.

Yield on a zero-coupon bond

Zero-coupon bonds, sometimes known as *strips*, have only one cash flow,
the redemption payment on maturity. Typically this payment will be par
(100) and hence the bond is sold at a discount to par and trades at a
discount during its life. For a bond with only one cash flow it is obviously
not necessary to use (2.4) and instead we can use (2.8) as stated below.

$$P = \frac{C}{(1 + r)^{n}} \tag{2.8}$$

Equation (2.8) above substitutes n for S: n is the number of years to the
bond's redemption. We can rearrange the equation for the yield, r.

$$r = \left(\frac{C}{P}\right)^{\frac{1}{n}} - 1 \tag{2.9}$$

Index-linked yields

In certain markets including the US and UK markets, the government and
certain companies issue bonds that have either or both of their coupon and
principal linked to a price index, such as the retail price index (RPI), the
main measure of inflation. If we wish to calculate the yield on such *TIPS*
or *index-linked bonds* it is necessary to make forecasts of the relevant
index, which are then used in the yield calculation. As an example we can
use the index-linked government bonds that were first introduced in the UK
in March 1981. Both the principal and coupons on UK index-linked gilts
are linked to the RPI and are therefore designed to give a constant *real*
yield. Most of the index-linked stocks that have been issued by the UK
government have coupons of 2 or 2½ per cent. Apparently this was because
of the fact that the long-run real rate of return on UK capital stock is about
2½ per cent.

Both the coupon and the principal on index-linked gilts are scaled up by
the ratio of two values of the RPI. The denominator of this ratio is known

as the *base RPI* and is the value of the RPI eight months prior to the month of the issue of the bond. The numerator is the value of the RPI eight months prior to the month of the relevant coupon or principal payment.

The semi-annual coupon payment is given by 2.10 below.

$$\text{Coupon payment} = (C/2) \times \frac{RPI_{m-8}}{RPI_b} \qquad (2.10)$$

The principal repayment is given by 2.11.

$$\text{Principal repayment} = 100 \times \frac{RPI_{m-8}}{RPI_b} \qquad (2.11)$$

where *C* is the *real* annual coupon payment and where

RPI_b is the value of RPI eight months prior to the month of issue (the base RPI)

RPI_{m-8} is the value of RPI eight months prior to the month in which coupon is paid

RPI_{M-8} is the value of RPI eight months prior to the month of bond redemption.

The eight-month lag in the RPI is used for the following reason. The authorities require to know each coupon payment six months before it is paid in order to determine the interest accruing between coupon payments. The two additional months are explained by the one-month delay in publishing the RPI (for example, June's RPI is not published until July) and an allowance of one month to make the relevant calculations. It is also important to take into account any rebasing of the RPI. The index was last rebased in January 1987, to 100 from the January 1974 value of 394.5.

Example 2.4

Index-linked Treasury 2% 1988 was issued in March 1982 and matured on 30 March 1988. The base RPI was 297.1 (that is, the RPI for July 1981); the RPI for July 1987 was 101.8. Thus we can calculate the money value of the final coupon payment and principal repayment on 30 March 1988 as shown below.

$$\text{Coupon payment} = (2/2) \times \frac{394.5}{297.1} \times \frac{101.8}{100.0} = £1.3517$$

$$\text{Principal repayment} = 100 \times \frac{394.5}{297.1} \times \frac{101.8}{100.0} = £135.1736$$

The interest accruing during the last coupon period (30 September 1987–30 March 1988) can be calculated once we know the final coupon payment, given below.

$$1.3517 \times \frac{\text{No. of days accrued}}{(365/2)}$$

There are two kinds of index-linked yields to maturity: the money (or nominal) yield, and the real yield. The money yield requires forecasts of all future cash flows from the bond. This in turn requires forecasts of all the relevant future RPIs. The commonest way of doing this is to take the latest available RPI and assume a constant inflation rate thereafter.

The forecast for the first relevant future RPI is determined using (2.12):

$$RPI_1 = RPI_0 \times (1 + \tau)^{m/12} \tag{2.12}$$

where

RPI_0 is the latest available RPI
τ is the forecast of the annual inflation rate
m is the number of months between RPI_0 and RPI_1.

Suppose for instance that the bond pays coupons every March and September. The relevant months for forecasting the RPI are eight months prior to March and September, namely July and January. If the latest available RPI is for October, then we are attempting to make a forecast for the RPI the following January, in which case $m = 3$. The forecast for each subsequent relevant RPI is found using (2.13):

$$RPI_{j+1} = RPI_1 \times (1 + \tau)^{j/12} \tag{2.13}$$

where j is the number of semi-annual forecasts after RPI_1 (which was the forecast for the RPI in January). For example if the October RPI is 102.8 and an annual inflation rate of 4.5 per cent is expected, then the forecast for the RPI for the following January is

$$RPI_1 = 102.8 \times (1.045)^{3/12}$$
$$= 103.9$$

and for the January following that it is

$$RPI_3 = 103.9 \times (1.045)$$
$$= 108.6$$

The *money yield* (rm) is calculated by solving the following equation, assuming that the calculation is made on a coupon payment date, so that accrued interest is zero:

$$P_d = \frac{(C/2)(RPI_1/RPI_b)}{(1 + \frac{1}{2}rm)} + \frac{(C/2)(RPI_2/RPI_b)}{(1 + \frac{1}{2}rm)^2} + ... + \frac{(C/2 + M)(RPI_S/RPI_b)}{(1 + \frac{1}{2}rm)^S}$$

$$(2.14)$$

where S is the number of coupon payments before redemption.

The *real yield* (ry) is related to the money yield through equation 2.24, which was first described by Fisher in his theory of interest (1930):

$$(1 + \frac{1}{2}ry) = (1 + \frac{1}{2}rm) / (1 + \tau)^{\frac{1}{2}}$$

$$(2.15)$$

For example if the money yield is 7 per cent and the forecast inflation rate is 4.5 per cent, then the real yield is found from (2.15) as shown.

$$ry = \left\{ \frac{[1 + \frac{1}{2}(0.007)]}{[1 + (0.045)]^{\frac{1}{2}}} - 1 \right\} \times 2$$

$$\cong 0.025 \ (2.5\%)$$

Equation (2.14) is used to show that the money yield is the appropriate discount rate for discounting money or nominal cash flows, and can be rearranged to show that the real yield is the appropriate discount rate for discounting real cash flows.

To compare returns between index-linked bonds and conventional bonds it is necessary to calculate the *break-even inflation rate*. This is the inflation rate that makes the money yield on an index-linked bond equal to the redemption yield on a conventional bond of the same maturity. Suppose that the redemption yield on a conventional bond is 5 per cent and that the real return on an index-linked bond is 2.5 per cent. Using (2.15) this gives us a break-even inflation rate of:

$$\tau = \left\{ \frac{[1 + \frac{1}{2}(0.05)]}{[1 + \frac{1}{2}(0.025)]} \right\}^2 - 1$$

$$= 0.02484 \ (2.48\%)$$

If the expected rate of inflation is higher than the break-even rate of inflation, investors will prefer the index-linked bond, and vice versa.

The price/yield relationship

The foregoing analysis has illustrated a fundamental property of bonds, namely that an upward change in the price results in a downward move in the yield, and vice versa. This is of course immediately apparent since the price is the present value of the cash flows; as the required yield for a bond decreases, say, the present value and hence the price of the cash flow for the bond will increase. It is also reflects the fact that for plain vanilla bonds the coupon is fixed, therefore it is the price of the bond that will need to fluctuate to reflect changes in market yields. It is useful sometimes to plot the relationship between yield and price for a bond. A typical price/yield profile is represented graphically in Figure 2.3, which shows a convex curve.

As we have said, for a plain vanilla bond with a fixed coupon, the price is the only variable that can change to reflect changes in the market environment. When the coupon rate of a bond is equal to the market rate, the bond price will be par (100). If the required interest rate in the market moves above a bond's coupon rate at any point in time, the price of the bond will adjust downward in order for the bondholder to realise the additional return required. Similarly if the required yield moves below the coupon rate, the price will move up to equate the yield on the bond to the market rate. As a bond will redeem at par, the capital appreciation realised on maturity acts as compensation when the coupon rate is lower than the market yield.

The price of a bond will move for various reasons, including the market-related ones noted here:

- when there is a change in the yield required by the market, either because of changes in the central bank base rate or a perceived change in credit

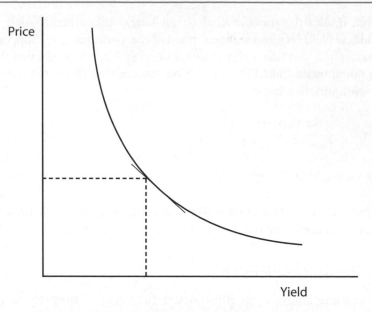

Figure 2.3 The bond price/yield relationship

quality of the bond issuer (credit considerations do not affect developed country government bonds)

- when there is a change because as the bond is approaching maturity, its price moves gradually towards par
- when there is a change in the market-required yield because of a change in the yield on comparable bonds.

Bond prices also move for liquidity reasons and normal supply and demand reasons, for example if there is a large amount of a particular bond in issue it is easier to trade the bond; also if there is demand due to a large customer base for the bond. *Liquidity* is a general term used here to mean the ease with which a market participant can trade in or out of a position. If there is always a ready buyer or seller for a particular bond, it will be easier to trade in the market.

So we know now the following:

- If the yield rises, the price of the bond goes down.
- If the yield falls, the price of the bond goes up
- If the price of the bond is below par (100), the coupon is lower than the yield, and if the price is above par, then the coupon is above the yield.

Good stuff. Let's move on.

MORE QUEASY STUFF: A (THANKFULLY!) BRIEF WORD ON DURATION

It's worth spending just a bit of time on the subject of duration, and the concept of interest rate risk. Private investors don't need to get too bogged down in this area, just as long as they are aware of it.

One of the key identifying features of a bond is its term to maturity. However this does not tell us the full story on the timing of the bond's cash flows, or its price behaviour in the market compared with other bonds. All bonds, except zero-coupon bonds, pay part of their total return during their lifetime, in the form of coupon interest, so that the term to maturity does not reflect the true period over which the bond's return is earned. Also if we wish to gain an idea of the trading characteristics of a bond, and compare this with other bonds of similar maturity, the term to maturity is insufficient and so we need a more accurate measure.[3]

Revisiting the bond price/yield relationship

Earlier we showed how for a plain vanilla bond, because the coupon is fixed, the price is the only parameter of the bond's make-up that can change in response to a change in market interest rates. Hence a bond's price will move in the opposite direction from a move in market interest rates, where the latter has triggered a change in the required yield for that bond. The extent of the change in bond price will depend on how sensitive the bond is to interest rate changes. This is different for different bonds. For example, Figure 2.4 shows the price/yield relationship for three bonds of differing maturities and coupons: this illustrates how the nature of the convex relationship between price and yield is different for each bond.

From Figure 2.4 note that the change in price for a given in change in interest rates (see the change along the x-axis) is not uniform for an upward or downward change in yield. If we measure the change along the price axis for a fixed change in the yield axis, we can see most obviously for the 11% 2019 bond that the price increase is greater than the price decrease for a given in change in yield. This is observed for all bonds where the price/yield relationship is convex. We can also see from Figure 2.4 that the 5% 2002 bond is less convex than the 11% 2019 bond; so while the property of upward price changes outstripping downward price changes still holds, it is less obvious than for the longer-dated bond.

What is the significance of this? Essentially, private investors should be aware that certain bonds are more 'risky', from an interest-rate change point of view, than others. If you buy a bond with the intention of holding

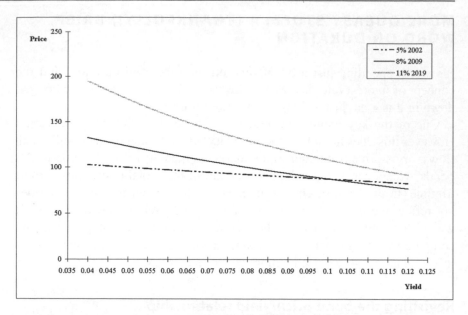

Figure 2.4 Price/yield relationship for three hypothetical bonds, as at October 1999

it until maturity, you will not be concerned with its level of interest rate risk, but you might be more comfortable holding bonds of lower interest rate risk. You can get an idea of the extent of this risk from *duration* or *modified duration*.

Duration

A plain vanilla coupon bond pays out a proportion of its return during the course of its life, in the form of coupon interest. If we were to analyse the properties of a bond, we should conclude quite quickly that its maturity gives us little indication of how much of its return is paid out during its life, and no idea of the timing or size of its cash flows, and hence its sensitivity to moves in market interest rates. For example, if we compare two bonds with the same maturity date but different coupons, the higher coupon bond provides a larger proportion of its return in the form of coupon income than does the lower coupon bond. The higher coupon bond provides its return at a faster rate; its value is theoretically therefore less subject to subsequent fluctuations in interest rates.

We may wish to calculate an average of the time to receipt of a bond's cash flows, and use this measure as a more realistic indication of maturity. However cash flows during the life of a bond are not all equal in value, so a more accurate measure would be to take the average time to receipt of a bond's cash flows, but weighted in the form of the cash flows' present value. This is, in effect, *duration*. We can measure the speed of payment of a bond, and hence its price risk relative to other bonds of the same maturity, by measuring the average maturity of the bond's cash flow stream. Bond analysts use duration to measure this property. (It is sometimes known as Macaulay's duration, after its inventor, who first introduced it in 1938.[4])

Duration is the weighted average time until the receipt of cash flows from a bond, where the weights are the present values of the cash flows, measured in years. At the time that he introduced the concept, Macaulay used the duration measure as an alternative for the length of time that a bond investment had remaining to maturity.

We can illustrate Macaulay duration with a simple example, using a hypothetical five-year bond with precisely five years to maturity and a coupon of 8 per cent. Assume that the bond is priced at par, giving a yield to maturity of 8 per cent. The bond's cash flows are shown in Table 2.1, along with a diagram of the timing of cash flows as Figure 2.5.

The present value of each cash flow is calculated in the normal way, hence for the period 2 cash flow of £8 the present value is $8 / (1.08)^2$, which gives us 6.859. So we see that duration is then calculated using (2.16) below.

$$D = \frac{\Sigma(\text{present value of cash flow} \times \text{time to cash flow})}{\Sigma(\text{present value of cash flow})} \qquad (2.16)$$

TABLE 2.1 Example of duration calculation			
8% five-year bond, priced at par			
Cash flow	**Present value (PV)***	**Timing (t)**	**PV × t**
8.00	7.41	1	7.41
8.00	6.86	2	13.72
8.00	6.35	3	19.05
8.00	5.88	4	23.52
108.00	73.5	5	367.51
	100.0		431.21
* calculated as C(1 + r)t			
Duration is the sum of all PV × t divided by P, = 431.21/100 or 4.31 years.			

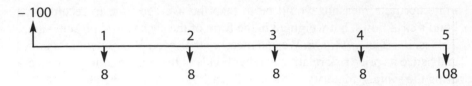

Figure 2.5 Receipt of cash flows for an 8% five-year bond

Mathematically this is written as (2.17) below.[5]

$$D = \frac{\sum_{n=1}^{N} \dfrac{nC_n}{(1 + r)^n}}{P} \tag{2.17}$$

where

D is the Macaulay duration
C is the bond cash flow at time n
P is the present value of the n-period cash flow, discounted at the current yield to maturity
n is the number of interest periods.

Note that the denominator, as the sum of all the present values of the cash flows, is in fact the price of the bond.

For a semi-annual coupon bond, the cash flows are discounted at half the current yield to maturity. Equation (2.17) solves for Macaulay duration in terms of the number of interest periods; we divided this by the number of interest periods per year (either 1 or 2 for annual or semi-annual coupon bonds) to obtain the Macaulay duration in years.

In our illustration of the 8% five-year bond, shown in Table 2.1, duration is calculated as 431.21/100, which is equal to 4.31 years. This implies that the average time taken to receive the cash flows on this bond is 4.31 years. This is shown in Figure 2.6 in our 'duration fulcrum', with 4.31 years being the time to the pivot, marked from A to B. The coupons are shown as 'C', and these diminish progressively as their present value decreases.

For a zero-coupon bond, where the present value of the coupon payments is zero because there are no coupon payments, the Macaulay duration can be shown to be equal to the number of interest periods remaining in the bond's life. If the bond is trading in a bond market with an annual

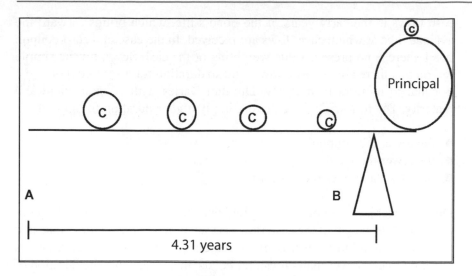

Figure 2.6 The duration fulcrum

coupon convention, the Macaulay duration is therefore equal to the number of years remaining to maturity.

In the appendix we show how you can use Microsoft Excel to calculate a bond's duration. It is a very straightforward procedure.

Market professionals commonly use a measure of bond price sensitivity to interest rates known as modified duration.[6] This is given as:

$$MD = \frac{D}{(1 + r)} \qquad (2.18)$$

Modified duration is clearly related to duration, but is a much more useful measure of risk. We can use it to indicate that, for small changes in yield, a given change in yield results in an inverse change in bond price. The modified duration value of a bond shows how much the price of the bond changes for a 1 per cent change in its yield. At this stage, I must point out that the duration and modified duration concept assume a number of factors, all of which are useless for the real world, most notably the assumption of a *parallel shift* in yields, but we don't have to worry about that here.

Properties of duration

Let us examine some of the properties of duration. A bond's duration is always less than its maturity. This is because some weight is given to the cash flows in the early years of the bond's life, which brings forward the average time at which cash flows are received. In the case of a zero-coupon bond, there is no present value weighting of the cash flows, for the simple reason that there are no cash flows, and so duration for a zero-coupon bond is equal to its term to maturity. Duration varies with coupon, yield and maturity. The following three factors imply *higher* duration for a bond:

- the lower the coupon
- the lower the yield
- broadly, the longer the maturity.

Duration increases as coupon and yield decrease. As the coupon falls, more of the relative weight of the cash flows is transferred to the maturity date and this causes duration to rise. Because the coupon on index-linked bonds is generally much lower than on vanilla bonds, this means that the duration of index-linked bonds will be much higher than for vanilla bonds of the same maturity. As yield increases, the present values of all future cash flows fall, but the present values of the more distant cash flows fall relatively more than those of the nearer cash flows. This has the effect of increasing the relative weight given to nearer cash flows and hence of reducing duration.

What is the upshot of all this? It is this: if you are intending to hold a bond for less than its full term to maturity (and given that investment decisions must always be flexible, to react to new information or a change in your personal circumstances), if you think that base interest rates are going to rise, you should hold bonds of lower duration, *all else being equal*. In other words, it is all right to compare duration of different gilts, because they have the same (zero) credit risk. You should never, as a private investor, hold a bond for duration reasons only. Put it this way: if you think interest rates are going to fall, and you have already decided to invest some of your funds in gilts, then there is no harm in buying a longer-dated gilt. If you think rates are going to rise, you should get a shorter-dated gilt. But either way, you are going to buy a gilt: you are just letting the duration concept influence your choice of which gilt to buy.

APPENDIX 2.1: USING MICROSOFT EXCEL® TO CALCULATE BOND YIELD AND DURATION

Figure 2.7 is an Excel worksheet showing gross redemption yield calculation and duration calculation for a 5% 2012 semi-annual coupon conventional bond, settlement date 5 November 2002. The duration calculation uses the bond yield in the formula, which is cell D12, and which was calculated first.

	Yield to maturity calculation	
	Column C	**Description**
Row 3	05/11/2002	Settlement date
4	07/11/2012	Maturity date
5	5.00%	Coupon
6	98.95	Price
7	£100	Redemption value
8	2	Coupon frequency (see below)
9	1	Accrued interest basis (see below)
	Formula	**Result**
	=YIELD(C3, C4, C5, C6, C7, C8, C9)	0.0514
		To view the result as a percentage, adjust the format to "percentage" using the Format and Cells menus.
	Coupon frequency	
	Annual = 1, Semi-annual = 2, Quarterly = 4	
	Accrued interest	
	US 30/360 = 0	
	Actual / actual = 1	
	Actual / 360 = 2	
	Actual / 365 = 3	
	European 30/360 = 4	
	Duration calculation	
	Formula	
	=DURATION(C3, C4, C5, D12, C8, C9)	7.785688677
		The duration of the same bond above, with yield of 5.14%.

Figure 2.7 Using Microsoft Excel® to calculate bond yield and duration

Notes

1 We look closer at yields a little later.
2 You will sometimes read that Eurobonds are bonds that are issued in a different currency from that of the issuer, but this is incorrect. The true definition is a bond that is issued in the international capital markets, usually by a syndicate of banks, and 'cleared' (settled) in the either of the two main clearing systems for Eurobonds, Euroclear and Clearstream.
3 By 'trading characteristics' we mean how a bond's price will change as a result of a change of market interest rates, compared with how the price of other bonds will change for the same movement in interest rates.
4 Macaulay, F., *Some theoretical problems suggested by the movements of interest rates, bond yields and stock prices in the United States since 1865*, National Bureau of Economic Research, NY, 1938. This is actually quite a fascinating read and can be bought today, published by the RISK Classics Library.
5 This assumes the bond has a whole number of interest periods to maturity; if this is not the case we round down to the nearest whole number.
6 Bond price sensitivity to interest rates is referred to as *interest rate sensitivity* or interest rate *risk*.

CHAPTER 3

The UK gilt market

I'm a big fan of gilts. In fact if it wasn't for the need to make this book a bit more complete, I'd be happy to just finish with this chapter. Most private investors will find that their fixed income investment needs are met by gilts. Or, like the author, you could add one or two building society permanent interest-bearing shares (PIBS) to your gilt holdings to add spice, and that would be it – perfect!

Gilts are bonds issued by the UK government. The term 'gilt' comes from *gilt-edged securities*, the official term for UK government bonds.[1] Gilts are the main method by which the UK government finances the short-fall between its expenditure and its tax revenues, and as they are direct obligations of the government they are the highest-rated securities in the sterling markets. Their AAA-rating reflects in part the fact that the UK government has never defaulted on an interest payment or principal repayment in the history of the gilt market, as well as the strength and standing of the UK economy. The market is also at the centre of the sterling financial asset markets and forms the basis for pricing of all other sterling assets and financial instruments. As well as being safe investments, gilts are also useful investments. They outperformed equities in 1998 and again in 2001. That's a bit like the chap entered for the steeplechase at your school sports day also winning the 100 metres sprint: a bit of a bonus, because gilts hold none of the risk of equities.

At the end of September 2002 there were 60 individual gilt issues in existence, representing nearly £242 billion nominal of debt outstanding. The majority of these are conventional fixed interest bonds, but there are also index-linked, double-dated and irredeemable gilts. Gilts are identified by their coupon rate and year of maturity; they are also given names such as *Treasury* or *Exchequer*. There is no significance attached to any particular name, all gilts are equivalent irrespective of their name.

Some gilts exist only in small quantities and are known as *rump* gilts. A full list of all gilts as at September 2005 is given in Appendix 3.1. The UK government issues gilts to finance its income deficit, previously known as the Public Sector Borrowing Requirement but now known as the Public Sector

Debt Requirement. The actual financing requirement each fiscal year is known as the Central Government Net Cash Requirement (CGNCR). The CGNCR, being the difference between central exchequer income and expenditure, always reflects a borrowing requirement except on rare occasions when the central government runs a surplus, as in 1988 and in 1998. New issues of debt are also made to cover repayment of maturing gilts.

The responsibility for issuing gilts rests with the Debt Management Office (DMO), an executive agency of Her Majesty's Treasury. The DMO is in charge of sterling debt management for the government. This transfer of duties traditionally performed by the Bank of England (BoE) was introduced after the Chancellor of the Exchequer handed over control of UK monetary policy to a committee of the bank, the Monetary Policy Committee, in May 1997. The DMO was set up in 1998 and assumed its responsibilities on 1 April 1998. Over the few years prior to this the gilt market had been subject to a series of reforms in its structure and operation, overseen by the BoE, designed to make gilts more competitive as investment instruments and to bring the market up to date. Recent innovations have included the introduction of an open market in gilt repo and a new market in zero-coupon bonds known as gilt *strips*, as well as improvements to the auction process. This included introduction of an auction calendar and a policy of building up large-volume, liquid benchmark issues.

Is this of relevance to private investors? Insofar as it reassures them that the market will continue to function as a liquid and efficient one, yes, but otherwise no – we need only be comfortable about the concept of investing in gilts.

INTRODUCTION AND HISTORY

UK national debt dates from 1694 when the government of King William raised £1.2 million in order to finance a war against France. The Bank of England was founded the following year. The currency itself however dates from much earlier than this, for instance the word *pondus* was a Latin word meaning 'weight' but signified the weight of the coin of money; while the '£' sign originates from the designation for 'libra', used to denote the pound. The term sterling originates from 'esterling', silver coins introduced during the reign of King Henry II in the twelfth century.[2] From this beginning the UK national debt has grown steadily, experiencing rapid growth during the wars in 1914–18 and 1939–45. Steady growth in national debt was observed in all developed economies in the post-war period.

As the gilt market forms the cornerstone of the sterling asset markets, the gilt yield curve is the benchmark for banks and corporates when setting interest rates and borrowing funds. As is common in many countries, government bonds in the UK form the largest sector within the UK bond markets; in September 2002 the nominal value outstanding comprised just over 51 per cent of the total nominal value of UK bonds. This figure was also larger than the total volume of sterling Eurobonds in issue at that time, approximately £200 billion. The remainder was made up of domestic bonds such as *debentures* and *bulldogs*.

Figure 2.2 (page 21) is an extract from the *Financial Times* showing prices and yields for the main benchmark conventional and index-linked gilts in issue.

MARKET INSTRUMENTS

Conventional gilts

The gilt market is essentially plain vanilla in nature. The majority of gilt issues are conventional fixed interest bonds. Conventional gilts have a fixed coupon and maturity date. By volume they made up 76 per cent of the market in September 2002. Coupon is paid on a semi-annual basis. The coupon rate is set in line with market interest rates at the time of issue, so the range of coupons in existence reflects the fluctuations in market interest rates Unlike many government and corporate bond markets, gilts can be traded in the smallest unit of currency, and frequently nominal amounts change hands in amounts quoted down to one penny (£0.01) nominal size. Individual gilts are given names such as the 7% Treasury 2002 or the 9% Conversion 2011. There is no significance attached to the name given to a gilt, and they all trade in the same way; most issues in existence are now 'Treasury' issues, although in the past it was sometimes possible to identify the purpose behind the loan by its name. For example a 'Conversion' issue usually indicates a bond converted from a previous gilt. The 3% Gas 1995/98 was issued to finance the nationalisation of the gas industry and was redeemed in 1998.

Gilts are registered securities. All gilts pay coupon to the registered holder as at a specified record date; the record date is seven business days before the coupon payment date. The period between the record date and the coupon date is known as the *ex-dividend* or 'ex-div' ('xd') date; during the ex-dividend period the bond trades without accrued interest. This is illustrated in Figure 3.1.

Bonds

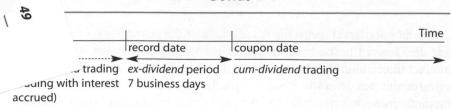

Figure 3.1 Gilt ex-dividend trading

The ex-dividend period was reduced from three weeks to seven business days for all gilts in 1998; the facility to trade *special ex-div*, which was a two-week period prior to the start of the ex-dividend period during which transactions could be traded ex-dividend on agreement between buyer and seller, was also removed in 1998. The ex-dividend period for one issue, 3½% War Loan, was retained at three weeks because of the large number of retail holders of this bond.

Index-linked gilts

The other major gilt instruments are *index-linked* (I-L) gilts, or 'linkers'. The UK was one of the first countries to introduce index-linked government bonds, with an issue in 1981. I-L gilts are designed to provide investors with an inflation-protected, real return from their bondholding. In September 2002 approximately 19 per cent of gilts in issue were linkers. I-L gilts link both their coupon and redemption payments to the UK retail price index (RPI), and this adjustment should in theory preserve the real value of investors' income and capital, independent of the rate of inflation. The RPI figure for eight months prior to the relevant cash flow is used to adjust the final value of each payment as it becomes due. To adjust a coupon payment therefore, the nominal value (this is the coupon rate) is adjusted using the RPI value recorded eight months prior to the bond's issue date and the RPI value recorded eight months prior to the coupon payment date.

The use of an earlier RPI index level, known as an 'indexation lag', is because the actual cash flow needs to be known six months before it is paid, so enabling the accrued interest on the bond to be calculated during the interest period. This accounts for six months of the lag, while RPI figures themselves are always issued one month after the month to which they relate (for instance, September's RPI is issued in October). The final redemption is treated in the same way. The existence of this indexation lag means that in practice I-L gilt returns are not completely protected from inflation.

The coupon level for I-L gilts is typically 2 per cent or 2½ per cent, which is lower than conventional gilts issued since the 1950s. This reflects the fact that, as the coupon is protected from inflation, the nominal coupon value is the real interest rate expected during the bond's life. Historically the real return on gilt stock has been around 2–3 per cent. The importance of indexed gilts in the market as a whole reflects the attraction that such debt has for *institutional* investors. While it might be of value for private investors, in the current low inflationary environment it is perhaps less useful. Since the establishment of the Monetary Policy Committee (MPC) and granting of operational independence to the Bank of England in 1997, there are good reasons for thinking that inflation should not be a problem barring external shocks, and so index-linked gilts should continue to be of less interest to private investors than conventional gilts.

The yield spread between I-L and conventional gilts fluctuates over time and is influenced by a number of factors and not solely by the market's view of future inflation (the implied forward inflation rate). The market uses this yield spread to gauge an idea of future inflation levels. The other term used to describe the yield spread is *breakeven inflation*, that is, the level of inflation required that would equate nominal yields on I-L gilts with yields on conventional gilts.

Example 3.1: real yields versus conventional gross redemption yields

On 10 October 1999 the 2% I-L Treasury 2006 gilt is trading at £231.90, a real yield of 2.209 per cent (assuming an inflation rate of 3 per cent). A double-dated gilt, the 3½% Funding 1999–2004, is trading at £92.72 which is equivalent to a gross redemption yield of 5.211 per cent, assuming the stock is redeemed at the final maturity date. A private investor currently holding the I-L gilt is recommended by her stockbroker to switch into the double-dated issue. The investor is a higher-rate taxpayer, and there is no capital gains tax to pay on gilt investments. Do you agree with the stockbroker's recommendation? What reasons lie behind your decision?

In order to compare the two gilts we need to make an assumption about future inflation. The yield spread between the two bonds implies a forward inflation rate of just over 3 per cent. Therefore if the actual inflation rate to 2004 averages more than 3 per cent, the investor would have been better served by the I-L gilt. At a price of

£92.72 the conventional gilt offers a capital gain on maturity of £7.28. The coupon on the investment is only 3.50 per cent, however. Compare this with an expected coupon of 4.50 per cent for the I-L bond, if we assume that inflation will stay at or around the MPC's target rate of 2.5 per cent. On maturity however the price of the I-L gilt will be £196.00, which we calculate using the current RPI level until maturity (this gives us 165.1 × 1.0257) and assuming 2.5 per cent inflation to 2006. This will result in a capital loss for the investor. As there is income tax to pay on gilts, the conventional gilt probably then is the better option for the investor who will pay tax at the higher rate on the coupon income.

However there are a range of factors for the investor to consider, and the most significant is the extent to which she wishes to protect herself against unexpected inflation. The final decision must also consider the investor's portfolio as a whole; for example a high level of cash holdings would imply a greater exposure to inflation, which would swing the argument in favour of holding I-L gilts.

Comparing the yield levels on indexed bonds across markets enables analysts to assess the inflation expectations in several countries at once. While this is carried out frequently, it is important to factor in the non-inflation expectation considerations that make up bond yields. A high level of demand for I-L bonds, or an overvalued conventional bond market, can sometimes imply a lower forward inflation rate than is realistic.

Double-dated gilts

There are currently six double-dated gilts in existence, but they represent a small proportion of the market and have not been issued since the 1980s. Double-dated gilts have two maturity dates quoted, and under the terms of issue the government redeems them on any day between the first and second maturity dates, provided at least three months notice is given. As with callable bonds in the corporate market, the government will usually redeem a double-dated bond early if it is trading above par, since this indicates that the coupon on the bond is above the prevailing market interest rate. Where the price is below par the bond will be allowed to run to the final redemption date. An example of the latter is the 3½% Funding 1999–2004, which traded well below par and therefore was run to its final maturity date of 14 July 2004, although the government could have redeemed it at any point between 1999 and July 2004, providing it gave at least three months notice.

Double-dated issue are usually less liquid than conventional or I-L gilts, mainly because there is a relatively small amount in issue and also because a larger proportion are held by personal investors. They also tend to have high coupons, reflecting the market rates in existence at the time they were issued.

Floating rate gilts

In recent years the government has issued conventional floating rate gilts, the last of which matured in March 2001. Floating rate gilts pay coupon on a quarterly basis at the London Interbank Bid Rate (LIBID) minus 12.5 basis points. The BoE calculates the coupon level based on the LIBID fixing for the day before the coupon payment is due.[3] The liquidity of floating rate gilts is comparable to conventional gilts.

Gilt strips

Gilt strips are zero-coupon bonds created from conventional coupon gilts. Only issues actually designated as strippable gilts may be stripped. They are considered separately later in this chapter.

Undated gilts

The most esoteric instruments in the gilt market are the undated gilts, also known as *irredeemable gilts* or *consols*. These are very old issues; indeed some date from the nineteenth century.[4] There are eight such issues, and they do not have a maturity date. Redemption is therefore is at the discretion of the government. Some undated issues are very illiquid. The largest issue is the 3½% War Loan, with just over £1.9 billion in existence. In the past the BoE undertook conversions of the less liquid irredeemable bonds into War Loan, so that for all but this stock and the 2½% Treasury bond there are only *rump* amounts remaining. The government can choose to redeem an undated gilt provided a requisite notice period is given (this varies for individual issues but generally is three months), but in practice – given that the coupon on these bonds is very low – is unlikely to do so unless market interest rates drop below say 3 per cent. A peculiarity of three of the undated gilts is that they pay interest on a quarterly basis.[5]

Treasury bills

Strictly speaking Treasury bills (T-bills) are not part of the gilts market but form part of the sterling money markets. They are short-term government instruments, issued at a discount and redeemed at par. The most common bills are three-month (or 91-day) maturity instruments, although in theory any maturity between one-month and 12-month may be selected. In the past the BoE has issued one-month and six-month bills in addition to the normal three-month maturity bills. Bills are issued via a weekly tender at which anyone may bid. Generally clearing banks, building societies and *discount houses* take an active part in the bill market.

In debt capital markets the yield on a domestic government T-bill is usually considered to represent the *risk-free* interest rate, since it is a short-term instrument guaranteed by the government. This makes the T-bill rate, in theory at least, the most secure investment in the market. It is common to see the three-month T-bill rate used in corporate finance analysis and option pricing analysis, which often refer to a risk-free money market rate.

The responsibility for bill issuance was transferred to the DMO from the BoE in 1999. The DMO set up a slightly changed framework[6] in order to facilitate continued market liquidity. The main elements of the framework included a wider range of maturities and a larger minimum issue size at each weekly tender, plus a guaranteed minimum stock in issue of £5 billion. The DMO also pre-announces the maturities that will be available in the next quarter's tenders. The settlement of T-bills has been fixed at the next working day following the date of the tender.

Maturity breakdown of stock outstanding

Gilts are classified by the DMO and the *Financial Times* as 'shorts' if maturing in 0–7 years, 'mediums' if maturing in 7–15 years and 'longs' if maturing in over 15 years' time. Gilt-edged market makers (GEMMs) usually apply a different distinction, with shorts being classified as 0–3 years, mediums as 4–10 years and longs as those bonds maturing in over 10 years.

Market trading conventions

Gilts are quoted on a clean price basis, for next day settlement. This is known as 'cash' settlement or T+1.

Price quote

From 1 November 1998 gilt prices changed from pricing in *ticks* to pricing in decimals. (A tick is 1/32nd of a point; it was therefore equal to 0.03125. The tick price quote is employed in the US Treasury market.) Prices are now displayed as £ and pence per cent of stock. Auction bids are to two decimal places and gilt-edged market maker (GEMM) reference prices are up to four decimal places. The bid–offer spread is very close in the gilt market, reflecting its liquidity and transparency. For bonds up to ten years in maturity it is possible to receive quotes as narrow as £0.01 between bid and offer, although of course private investors will be quoted a wider spread.

Daycount convention

The accrued interest daycount convention for the calculation of accrued interest was changed from ACT/365 to ACT/ACT, from 1 November 1998. In Chapter 2 we showed how this results in slightly different results for the same number of days of accrued interest; however private investors need not be unduly concerned with this.

Market prices

Private investors can check the previous day's closing prices for gilts in the *Financial Times*. Gilt prices are not usually very volatile so these prices should be good enough for most dealing decisions. Prices can also be checked on the DMO's website, which is www.dmo.gov.uk and can be used to check historical prices.

INVESTING IN GILTS

It is very easy to buy and sell gilts. As a private investor, you can check prices and transact gilts at a *share shop*, or through certain accountants and solicitors. A share shop is a high street bank that has been set up with a terminal that allows instant share dealing. You can of course buy and sell gilts through your stockbroker. In addition it is perfectly legal for an individual to sell a gilt to another private investor, as long as the transaction is properly recorded. Prices and yields can be tracked from the *Financial Times* or a website such as the DMO's, which is very useful. The exact page address is

http://www.dmo.gov.uk/gilts/data/f3gem.htm

However as Leo Gough says in his book *How The Stock Market Really Works* (2001), the best way to buy and sell gilts is via the Royal Mail: in other words, by post. This service is provided by the Bank of England, and used to be known as the National Savings Stock Register but now appears to be called the Bank of England Brokerage Service. This is a straightforward process, and the Bank undertakes to transact orders on the day they are received, although this not guaranteed. Full information is available from the Bank's website, www.bankofengland.co.uk, and the actual page web link is

http://www.bankofengland.co.uk/Links/setframe.html

As well as the application forms, which can be downloaded as Adobe Acrobat files (.pdf), this site contains much useful information including a guide to investing in gilts, a list of dividend dates, commission rates, and sundry other details.[7] The commission rates are very good value for money compared with other broker rates, but of course the execution is not real-time.

TAXATION

Gilts are free of capital gains tax. Coupon interest is payable gross, without deduction of withholding tax. Investors who are resident in the UK for tax purposes are liable to pay income tax at their marginal rate on gilt coupons, however. Therefore interest received, including the inflation uplift on I-L gilts, must be declared on annual tax returns.

The tax treatment for resident private investors is summarised below.

Resident private investors

Individual private investors resident in the UK are liable for income tax on gilt coupon interest received. This includes accrued interest earned during a short-term holding. Capital gain made on a disposal of gilts is not liable to tax. Gains accruing on gilt strips are taxable, however, on an annual basis. Strip earnings are taxed as income on an annual basis, irrespective of whether the strip has actually been sold. That is, the tax authorities deem a strip to have been sold and repurchased at the end of the tax year, with any gain taxed as income. A savings vehicle introduced in April 1999, known as an Individual Savings Account (ISA), allows individuals to hold gilts free of both income and capital taxes. There is a limit on the amount that may be held, which is a maximum of £5,000 per annum from tax year

2000/01 onwards. Gilt strips may also be held free of tax in an ISA, within the £5,000 yearly limit.[8]

Overseas investors

Investors who are resident overseas, both corporate and individual, are exempt from UK tax on gilt holdings. Prior to April 1998 only gilts designated as 'Free of Tax to Residents Abroad' (FOTRA) paid gross coupons automatically to overseas residents; however from that date all gilts have been designated FOTRA stocks and thus overseas investors receive gross gilt coupons.

Unlike UK equity market transactions, there is no stamp duty or stamp duty reserve tax payable on purchases or sales of gilts.

MARKET STRUCTURE

The gilt market operates within the overall investment business environment in the UK. As such wholesale market participants are regulated by the Financial Services Authority (FSA), the central regulatory authority brought into being by the newly elected Labour government in 1997. The FSA regulates the conduct of firms undertaking business in the gilt market; it also supervises the exchanges on which trading in gilts and gilt derivatives takes place. The previous regulatory regime in the UK markets, as conducted under the Financial Services Act 1986, consisted of market participants being authorised by self-regulatory organisations such as the Securities and Futures Authority (SFA). The FSA was set up initially through merging all the different self-regulatory bodies. Hence gilt market makers (known as *gilt-edged market makers* or GEMMs) and brokers are authorised by the FSA. The FSA became the overall market regulator for all practitioners at the end of 2000.[9]

The gilt market is an 'over-the-counter' market, meaning that transactions are conducted over the telephone between market participants. However all individual issues are listed on the London Stock Exchange (LSE), which as a Recognised Investment Exchange is also supervised by the FSA.

MARKET MAKERS

Just as in the USA and France for example, there is a registered primary dealer system in operation in the UK government bond market. The present structure dates from 'Big Bang' in 1986, the large-scale reform of the London market that resulted in the abolition of the old distinction between *jobbers* and *brokers* and allowed firms to deal in both capacities if they so wished. It also resulted in stock and share trading moving off the floor of the Stock Exchange and into the dealing rooms of banks and securities houses. Firms that wished to provide a two-way dealing service and act on their own account registered as gilt-edged market makers. In 1986 there were 29 companies so registered, most of which were the gilts trading arms of the large banks. Firms registered as GEMMs with the Bank of England, and until 1998 there was a requirement for GEMMs to be separately capitalised if they were part of a larger integrated banking group. This requirement has since been removed. In September 2002 there were 16 firms registered as GEMMs, which must now be recognised as such by the DMO. GEMMs are also required to be members of the LSE.

The key obligation of GEMMs is to make two-way prices on demand in all gilts, thereby providing liquidity to the market. From his time working as a GEMM the author knows that some firms observe this requirement more closely than others! Certain gilts that the DMO has designated as rump stocks do not form part of this requirement.

In return for carrying out its market-making obligations, a GEMM receives certain privileges exclusive to it, which are:

- the right to make competitive telephone bids at gilt auctions and tap issues
- a reserved amount of stock at each auction, available at non-competitive bid prices (currently this is 0.5 per cent of the issue for each GEMM, or 10 per cent if an I-L gilt)
- access to the DMO's gilt dealing screens, through which the GEMM may trade or switch stocks
- a trading relationship with the DMO whenever it wishes to buy or sell gilts for market management purposes
- the facility to strip gilts
- a quarterly consultation meeting with the DMO, which allows the GEMM to provide input on which type of stocks to auction in the next quarter, plus advice on other market issues
- access to gilt inter-dealer broker (IDB) screens.

In 1998 the DMO set up a separate category of GEMMs known as index-linked GEMMs (IG GEMMs). A firm could opt for registration for either or both of the categories. The role of an IG GEMM is the same as for conventional GEMMs, applied to index-linked gilts. An IG GEMM has the same obligations as a GEMM with respect to I-L gilts, and an additional requirement that it must seek to maintain a minimum 3 per cent market share of the I-L gilt market. Therefore an IG GEMM must participate actively in auctions for I-L stock. In addition to the privileges listed above, IG GEMMs also have the right to ask the DMO to bid for any I-L gilt. In September 2002 eight of the 16 GEMMs were also registered as IG GEMMs.

Private investors do not deal with GEMMs.

The role of the Bank of England

Although the responsibility for UK government debt management has been transferred to the DMO, the BoE continues to maintain a link with the gilt market. The Bank is also involved in monitoring other sterling markets such as gilt futures and options, swaps, strips, gilt repo and domestic bonds. The Bank's *Quarterly Bulletin* for February 1999 listed its operational role in the gilt market as:

- Calculating and publishing the coupons for index-linked gilts, after the publication of each month's inflation data and inflation index.
- Setting and announcing the dividend for floating-rate gilts, which is calculated as a spread under three-month LIBID each quarter.
- Operating the BoE brokerage service, a means by which private investors can buy and sell gilts by post instead of via a stockbroker. This service was previously operated by National Savings, the governments savings bank for private retail customers. Private investors sometimes wish to deal in gilts by post as usually commission charges are lower and it is a user-friendly service.

This is in addition to the normal daily money market operations, which keep the Bank closely connected to the gilt repo market. The BoE's dealers also carry out orders on behalf of its customers, primarily other central banks.

The BoE has a duty to 'protect the interests of index-linked gilt investors' (DMO 1999). This is a responsibility to determine whether any future changes in the composition of the RPI index would be materially harmful to I-L gilt holders, and to effect a redemption of any issue, via HM Treasury, if it feels any change had been harmful.

ISSUING GILTS

Auctions are the primary means of issuance of all gilts, both conventional and index-linked. They are generally for £2–3 billion nominal of stock on

Bonds

a competitive bid price basis. Auctions of index-linked gilts are for between £0.5 billion and £1.25 billion nominal. The programme of auctions is occasionally supplemented in between auctions by sales of stock 'on tap'. This is an issue of a further tranche of stock of a current issue, usually in conditions of temporary excess demand in that stock or that part of the yield curve. That said, only one conventional stock has been tapped since 1996, a £400 million tap in August 1999. The DMO has stated that tap issues of conventional gilts will only take place in exceptional circumstances.

After an auction the authorities generally refrain from issuing stocks of a similar type or maturity for a 'reasonable' period. Such stock will only be issued if there is a clear demand.

The 1996/97 remit for gilt issuance was accompanied by changes to the structure for gilt auctions. These changes were designed to encourage participation in auctions and to make the process smoother. The average size of auctions was reduced and a monthly schedule put in place; periodic dual auctions were also introduced. Dual auctions allow the issue of two stocks of different maturity in the same month, which moderates the supply of any one maturity and also appeals to a wider range of investors. GEMMs were allowed to put in bids by telephone up to five minutes before the close of bidding for the auction, which allowed them to accommodate more client demand into their bids. Instituting a pre-announced auction schedule at the start of the fiscal year further assists market transparency and predictability in gilt auctions, which reduced market uncertainty. In theory a reduction in uncertain should result in lower yields over the long term, which reduce government borrowing costs.

The DMO has a slightly different auction procedure for I-L gilts. Unlike conventional gilts, which are issued through a multiple price auction, I-L gilts are auctioned on a uniform price basis. This reflects the higher risks associated with bidding for I-L stock. In an auction for a conventional gilt, a market maker will be able to use the yields of similar maturity stock currently trading in the market to assist in her bid; in addition a long position in the stock can be hedged using exchange-traded gilt futures contracts.

There is a very liquid secondary market in conventional gilts. For these reasons a market maker will be less concerned about placing a bid in an auction without knowing at what level other GEMMs are bidding for the stock. In an I-L gilt auction there is a less liquid secondary market and it is less straightforward to hedge an I-L gilt position. There are also fewer I-L issues in existence; indeed there may not be another stock anywhere near the maturity spectrum of the gilt being auctioned. The use of a uniform price auction reduces the uncertainty for market makers and encourages them to participate in the auction.

Auction procedure

As part of its government financing role, HM Treasury issues an auction calendar just before the start of the new financial year in April. The DMO provides further details on each gilt auction at the start of each quarter in the financial year, when it also confirms the auction dates for the quarter and the maturity band that each auction will cover. For example, the quarterly announcement might state that the auction for the next month will see a gilt issued of between four and six years maturity. Announcements are made via Reuters, Telerate and Bridge news screens. Eight days before the auction date the DMO announces the nominal size and the coupon of the stock being auctioned. If it is a further issue of an existing stock, the coupon obviously is already known. After this announcement, the stock is listed on the LSE and market makers engage in 'when issued' trading (also known as the *grey market*). When issued trading involves buying and selling stock to the forward settlement date, which is the business day after the auction date. As in the Eurobond market, when issued trading allows market makers to gauge demand for the stock amongst institutional investors, and also helps in setting the price on the auction day.

Conventional gilts

In conventional gilt auctions, bidding is open to all parties including private individuals. Institutional investors will usually bid via a GEMM. Only GEMMs can bid by telephone directly to the DMO.[10] Other bidders must complete an application form. Forms are made available in the national press, usually the *Financial Times*. This makes it easy for private investors to apply for new issue gilts. The application form allows you to specify either a nominal amount of stock, in which case you must send in an 'open' cheque with the form, or an actual amount of cash to invest.

For the market professionals, bidding can be competitive or non-competitive. In a competitive bid, participants bid for one amount at one price, for a minimum nominal value of £500,000. If a bid is successful the bidder will be allotted stock at the price it put in. There is no minimum price. Telephone bidding must be placed by 10.30 am on the morning of the auction and in multiples of £1 million nominal. Bidding is closed at 10.30 am. In a non-competitive bid, GEMMs can bid for up to 0.5 per cent of the nominal value of the issue size, while others can bid for up to a maximum of £500,000 nominal, with a minimum bid of £1,000. Non-competitive bids are allotted in full at the weighted-average of the successful competitive bid

price. In both cases, non-GEMMs must submit an application form either
to the BoE's registrar department or to the DMO, in both cases to arrive no
later than 10.30 am on the morning of the auction.

The results of the auction are usually announced by the DMO by 11.15
am. The results include the highest, lowest and average accepted bid
prices, the gross redemption yields for these prices, and the value of non-
competitive bids for both GEMMs and non-GEMMs. The DMO also
publishes important information on auction performance, which is used
by the market to judge how well the auction has been received. This
includes the difference between the highest accepted yield and the average yield of all accepted bids, known as the *tail,* and the ratio of bids
received to the nominal value of the stock being auctioned, which is
known as the *cover.* A well-received auction will have a small tail and
will be covered many times, suggesting high demand for the stock. A
cover of less than 1.5 times is viewed unfavourably in the market, and the
price of the stock usually falls on receipt of this news. A cover over two
times is well received.

On rare occasions the cover will be less than one, which is bad news for
the sterling bond market as a whole. A delay in the announcement of the
auction result is sometimes taken to be as a result of poor demand for the
stock. The DMO reserves the right not to allot the stock on offer, and it is
expected that this right might be exercised if the auction was covered at a
very low price, considerably discounted to par. The DMO also has the right
to allot stock to bidders at its discretion. This right is retained to prevent
market distortions from developing, for example if one bidder managed to
buy a large proportion of the entire issue. Generally the DMO seeks to
ensure that no one market maker receives more than 25 per cent of the issue
being auctioned for its own book.

Index-linked gilts

Auction bids for I-L gilts are also competitive and non-competitive. Only
IG GEMMs may make competitive bids, for a minimum of £1 million
nominal and in multiples of £1 million. For I-L gilts there is a uniform price
format, which means that all successful bidders receive stock at the same
price. A bid above the successful price will be allotted in full. Non-competitive bids must be for a minimum of £100,000, and will be allotted in full
at the successful bid price (also known as the 'strike' price). IG GEMMs
are reserved up to 10 per cent of the issue in the non-competitive bid facility. Non-IG GEMMs must complete and submit an application form in the
same way as for conventional gilt auctions.

The DMO reserves the right not to allot stock, and to allot stock to bidders at its discretion. The maximum holding of one issue that an IG GEMM can expect to receive for its own book is 40 per cent of the issue size.

Conversions

In the new reformed environment of the gilt market, the emphasis is on having a large, liquid supply of benchmark issues in existence. The BoE used conversion offers to switch holdings of illiquid gilts into more liquid benchmark stocks. The DMO has instituted a formal conversion programme. Conversion offers are made to bondholders to enable them to exchange (convert) their gilts into another gilt. The new gilt is usually the benchmark for that maturity. The aim behind conversion offers is to build up the issue size of a benchmark gilt more quickly than would be achieved by auctions alone, which are a function of the government's borrowing requirement. A period of low issuance as a result of healthy government finances would slow down the process of building up a liquid benchmark. By the same token, conversions also help to increase the size and proportion of strippable gilts more quickly. Conversions also, in the words of the DMO, concentrate liquidity across the yield curve by reducing the number of illiquid issues and converting them into benchmark issues. Illiquid gilts are usually high coupon issues with relatively small issue sizes. In the past for example, double-dated gilts have been converted into benchmark gilts.

Gilts that may be converted are usually medium and long-dated bonds with less than £5 billion nominal outstanding. The current distribution of a gilt is also taken into consideration: issues that are held across a wide range of investors, particularly private retail investors, are less likely to be offered for conversion for the reason that the offer will probably not be taken up widely.

HM Treasury and the DMO provide for liquid benchmark gilts at the 5, 10, 25 and 30-year maturity end of the yield curve. Conversion assists this process. The DMO uses the forward yield curve generated by its yield curve model in setting the terms of the conversion offer. The aim of the process is to make an offer to bondholders of the 'source' stock such that a large proportion of the stock is converted at a value fair to both the bondholder and the government.[11]

The conversion ratio is calculated using the dirty price of both source and 'destination' gilts. Both bond cash flows are discounted to the conversion date using the forward yield curve derived on the date of the conversion offer announcement. This approach also takes into account the 'pull to par' of both stocks; the running cost of funding a position in the source stock up to the conversion date is not taken into account. Conversion terms are announced three weeks before the conversion date, although an intention to convert will have been announced one or two weeks prior to this.

On announcement of the conversion terms, the DMO holds the fixed terms, in the form of a fixed price ratio of the two stocks, open for the three-week offer period. If the terms move in bondholders' favour they can convert, whereas if terms become unfavourable they may choose not to convert. It is not compulsory to take up a conversion offer. Holders of the source stock may choose to retain it and subsequently trade it, or hold it to maturity. However the source stock will become less liquid and less widely held after the conversion, more so if the offer is taken up in large quantities. If the remaining amount of the source stock is so small that it is no longer possible to maintain a liquid market in it, thereby making it a rump stock, GEMMs are no longer required to make a two-way price in it. Even if the stock does not end up as a rump issue, the bid–offer spread for it may widen. However these are not considerations if the investor is seeking to hold the bond to maturity. The DMO will announce if a stock acquires rump status; it also undertakes to bid for such stocks at the request of a market maker, as assistance towards the maintenance of an orderly market.

GILT STRIPS

Strips are the simplest type of bond in the market, because they have just one cash flow – the principal payment on maturity. As such they are zero-coupon bonds, and are *discounted* securities, because they are issued at a discount to their face value and then redeemed at par. They are ideal investments for private investors, because there are no coupon payments to worry about reinvesting, and they can be purchased with maturity dates to suit particular requirements.

Market mechanics

A strip is a zero-coupon bond, that is, a bond that makes no coupon payments during its life and has only one cash flow, its redemption payment on maturity. 'Stripping' a bond is the process of separating a standard coupon bond into its individual coupon and principal payments, which are then held separately and traded in their own right as zero-coupon bonds. For example a ten-year gilt can be stripped into 21 zero-coupon bonds, comprised of one bond from the principal repayment and 20 from the semi-annual coupons. Coupon payments due in 6, 12, 18 and so on months from the stripping date would become 6, 12, 18 and so on month zero-coupon bonds. The stripping process is carried out by a market maker – you don't have to worry about it.

You can buy strips via a stockbroker, but not through the post. This is because when strips were introduced the BoE believed that strips, which carried greater interest-rate risk than conventional gilts of similar maturity, should not be able to be purchased by retail investors unless they were aware of their characteristics, and the stockbroker plays the role of making them aware. This is unfortunate, because one of the handy things about gilts (well, conventional gilts) is that they can be bought and sold by post, directly with the government's National Savings arm. It is not too difficult to understand strips, so we can hope they become available through the post as well.

Strips are fully fledged gilts; they remain registered securities and liabilities of HM government, therefore they have identical credit risk to conventional gilts. Only gilts designated as strippable may be stripped: in fact all benchmark gilts are strippable. Since benchmark gilts are issued with coupon dates either on 7 June and 7 December or 7 March and 7 September, it means that strips are available with maturity dates every quarter, every year until 2055, the maturity year of the longest-dated gilt. This allows investors to match their investment timeframes easily with strips.

Stripped coupons from different gilts but with the same coupon dates are fully fungible; this increases their liquidity. At the moment there is no fungibility between coupon and principal strips, although this remains under review and may be possible at a later date.

A complete table of strip prices and yields can be viewed on the DMO's website.

Pricing convention

The BoE consulted with GEMMs before the introduction of the strips market on the preferred method for pricing strips. The result of this consultation was announced in May 1997, when the Bank stated that strips would trade on a yield basis rather than a price basis. The day count convention adopted, in both the conventional and strips market, was ACT/ACT.

It is handy for investors that strips are quoted in yield terms: they know exactly what yield they are getting. And unlike coupon bonds, the yield quoted for a strip is the true yield that will be received by the investor. Bear in mind that the yield is converted to a price when working out the total consideration (there is no accrued interest to worry about either). Remember that a fall in yields is good if you hold strips: it means that the price is going up. Of course, the price of the strip will gravitate slowly but surely to par, and will be par on its maturity date.

Interest rate risk for strips

Strips have a longer duration than equivalent maturity conventional bonds. As they are zero-coupon bonds their duration is equal in time to their maturity. The duration of a strip will decline roughly in parallel with time, whereas for a conventional bond the decline will be less. For a given modified duration, a strip will be less convex than a coupon bond. The following points highlight some of the salient points about how duration and convexity of strips compare with those of coupon bonds:

- Strips have a Macaulay duration equal to their time in years to maturity.
- Strips have a higher duration than coupon bonds of the same maturity.
- Strips are more convex than coupon bonds of the same maturity.
- Strips are less convex than coupon bonds of the same duration.

The reason that a strip is less convex than a conventional coupon bond of the same duration is that the coupon bond will have more dispersed cash flows than the strip. Although strips are less convex than bonds of identical duration, a high duration conventional gilt (6% Treasury 2028) had a duration of 15.56 years (modified duration 15.26) in March 1999, whereas the principal strip from that bond had a duration of 29.77 years at that time (modified duration 29.14). Long strips are therefore the most convex instruments in the gilt market.

Usefulness for private investors

Strips have a large number of uses for investors and traders. The following properties of strips make them potential attractive investments for investors:

- simplicity of one cash flow at maturity allows matching to future liabilities
- no reinvestment risk, as associated with conventional coupon-bearing bonds
- tax advantages if held within an ISA for UK investors.

Gilts are free of capital gains tax. However the Inland Revenue will treat strip price increases as income and will tax these under income tax rules for private investors. Therefore it is best to hold them within an ISA.

Strips are arguably the most basic cash flow structure available in the capital markets, as they are zero-coupon paper. By investing in a portfolio of strips an investor is able to construct a desired pattern of cash flows, one that matches more precisely his investment requirements than that obtained from a conventional bond. For instance, if you know that you will have a liability at some point in the future, say for college fees, you can invest in strips that mature at the required time. So where private investors wish to invest for a known future commitment, they can hold strips and realise the precise amount required at their investment horizon.

APPENDIX 3.1: LIST OF GILT STOCKS OUTSTANDING, 30 SEPTEMBER 2005

Conventional gilts	Redemption date	Amount in issue (£million)	Amount held in stripped form (£million)
8 ½% Treasury 2005	7 December 2005	10,486	191
7 ¾% Treasury 2006	8 September 2006	4,000	–
7 ½% Treasury 2006	7 December 2006	11,800	225
4 ½% Treasury 2007	7 March 2007	11,817	113
8 ½% Treasury 2007	16 July 2007	4,638	–
7¼% Treasury 2007	7 December 2007	11,100	134
5% Treasury 2008	7 March 2008	8,970	0
5 ½% Treasury 2008/2012	10 September 2008	1,000	–
4% Treasury 2009	7 March 2009	16,616	8
5 ¾% Treasury 2009	7 December 2009	8,937	22
4¾% Treasury 2009	7 June 2010	12,505	3
6 ¼% Treasury 2010	25 November 2010	4,958	–
9% Conversion 2011	12 July 2011	5,396	–
7 ¾% Treasury 2012/2015	26 January 2012	800	–
5% Treasury 2012	7 March 2012	13,346	– 0
8% Treasury 2013	27 September 2013	6,100	–
5% Treasury 2014	7 September 2014	13,410	2
4 ¾% Treasury 2015	7 September 2015	13,359	83
8% Treasury 2015	7 December 2015	7,377	399
8 ¾% Treasury 2017	25 August 2017	7,751	–
8% Treasury 2021	7 June 2021	16,740	268
5% Treasury 2025	7 March 2025	7,672	0
6% Treasury 2028	7 December 2028	11,756	172

4 ¼% Treasury 2032	7 June 2032	14,211	648
4 ¼% Treasury 2036	7 March 2036	15,338	255
4 ¾% Treasury 2038	7 December 2038	14,643	142
4 ¼% Treasury 2055	7 December 2055	4,750	–

Undated gilts

2 ½% Treasury	Undated	493	–
3 ½% War Loan	Undated	1,939	–

Index-linked gilts	Redemption date	Amount in issue (£million)	Nominal value including inflation uplift (£million)
2% I–L Treasury 2006	19 July 2006	2,037	5,166
2 ½% I–L Treasury 2009	20 May 2009	2,673	5,980
2 ½% I–L Treasury 2011	23 August 2011	3,942	9,317
2 ½% I–L Treasury 2013	16 August 2013	4,722	9,327
2 ½% I–L Treasury 2016	26 July 2016	6,055	13,072
2 ½% I–L Treasury 2020	16 April 2020	4,668	9,914
2 ½% I–L Treasury 2024	17 July 2024	5,400	9,744
4 1/8% I–L Treasury 2030	22 July 2030	3,171	4,136
1¼% I–L Treasury 2055	26 January 2035	7,222	7,859
2% I–L Treasury 2036	22 November 2055	1,250	1,250

'Ramp' gilts	Redemption date	Amount in issue (£million)
9 ¾% Conversion 2006	15 November 2006	6
9% Treasury 2008	13 October 2008	687
8% Treasury 2009	25 September 2009	393
9% Treasury 2012	6 August 2012	403
12% Exchequer 2013/2017	12 December 2013	58
2 ½% Annuities	Undated	3
3% Treasury	Undated	53
3 ½% Conversion	Undated	93
2 ½% Consolidated	Undated	275
2 ¾% Annuities	Undated	1
4% Consolidated	Undated	358

Double-dated issues currently trading above par are assumed to be called at first maturity.
(Source: DMO)

APPENDIX 3.2: RELATED GILT MARKET WEBSITES

UK Debt Management Office http://www.dmo.gov.uk
HM Treasury http://www.hm-treasury.gov.uk
Bank of England http://bankofengland.co.uk
LIFFE http://www.liffe.com
London Stock Exchange http://www.londonstockex.co.uk
Gilt investors http://www.gilt.co.uk

Notes

1   The legend is that the term 'gilt-edged' was used to refer to British government bonds because certificates representing individual bond holdings were originally edged with gold leaf or gilt. This tale is almost certainly apocryphal. Another commonly heard explanation is that UK government bonds were deemed to be as 'good as' (as safe as) gold, hence the term 'gilts'.
2   These and other fascinating facts are to be found in David Sinclair's splendid book *The Pound* (2000).
3   LIBID is the rate at which banks pay for funds they have borrowed from other banks.
4   For instance the 2½% Annuities gilt was issued in 1853. You won't find too many market makers who are keen to trade in it though!
5   These are 2½% Consolidated stock, 2½% Annuities and 2¾% Annuities.
6   This is set out in *The Future of UK Government Cash Management: The New Framework*, Debt Management Office, 4 December 1998.
7   You won't need the guide because you have this book!
8   We look at strips a little later.
9   This will be the Financial Services and Markets Act.
10 When telephoning one's bid, it is important to quote the correct 'big figure' for the stock! Sorry, Harry ...
11 The source stock is is the stock being converted out of.

CHAPTER 4

Investing in non-UK government bonds

Given the author's background, it should be no surprise that UK government bonds or gilts should already have been covered in depth and been thoroughly recommended to readers! However investors commonly invest in the government bonds of their own country, and more adventurous investors sometimes place some funds outside their own currency area. So in this chapter we discuss a few other country government markets.

Always remember that the gilt market is completely safe, and also very liquid and easy to deal in. This can only be said of a small number of government markets. The gilt market used to have a number of exotic features, which have gradually been removed so that its operation resembles that of other country markets such as the USA or Germany. While the passing of these features was mourned by old hands and others who had worked in the old market,[1] it has served to make gilts much more accessible to foreign investors. The markets discussed in this chapter are accessible to overseas investors to varying degrees.

OVERVIEW OF GOVERNMENT MARKETS

The primary market in government bonds

The size of government budget deficits has resulted in a steady increase in the size of public sector tradable debt over the last 20 years or so. During this time we have witnessed the emergence of a global, integrated capital market, which has resulted in a greater proportion of government bonds being held by foreign investors. The global investor base has increasingly been targeted by borrowing authorities, who see this as means of lowering borrowing costs. For instance in 2001 foreign investors held over 40 per cent of US government debt. This is a significant increase from the level of 15 years previously. This is by far the highest level among developed countries, although it has been increasing across all developed countries. The US figure also reflects that the US dollar is a reserve currency.

In recent years central authorities have implemented reforms to their market structure to help make their bonds more attractive to overseas investors. Reforms have typically been things such as paying of gross coupons, allowing international book-entry settlement (usually via international settlement or clearing institutions such as Euroclear and Clearstream), instituting pre-announced auction calendars, and greater transparency and liquidity in the secondary market.

One of the main reforms in government markets has been the introduction of auctions as the main method by which bonds are issued. Auctions are used in many developed and emerging government markets to issue debt, while corporate debt markets normally employ an underwriting *syndicate* to issue and place debt. The general understanding is that the auction method maximises revenue for the government. To facilitate greater transparency the issuing authorities release an *auction calendar* at the start of the fiscal year, which lists the government's proposed borrowing level and the approximate dates on which funds will be released. An auction calendar lowers the level of uncertainty for institutional investors, who are then in a better position to structure the maturity of their portfolios in line with the issuing calendar. The removal of uncertainty for market participants contributes to the success of a government bond auction.

Another innovation in government markets has been the concentration on benchmark issues. A specific large issue stock set as the benchmark issue will retain liquidity in the secondary market. If the market as a whole is comprised essentially of large-volume benchmark bonds it will be more liquid, and this helps to make it more transparent. The demand among institutional investors for benchmark issues may be observed in the yield curve; benchmark issues tend to trade around 10–20 basis points below the curve. For example Figure 4.1 and the table below show how the five-year, 10-year and 30-year benchmark gilts traded below other yields.

Investors prefer to hold benchmark bonds because the higher volume in issue tends to make them liquid and they have smaller bid–offer price spreads. The government also gains as the yield on benchmark issues is lower than other issues. The size of individual issues is important for smaller government bond markets, where there may not be enough investor demand to spread across a wide range of issues. This is a topical issue for emerging market economies. Benchmark bonds can be increased in size by auctioning further tranches at later dates, rather than issuing a new bond.

Another trend in government markets across the world has been an increase their 'user-friendly' level. Authorities frequently consult with

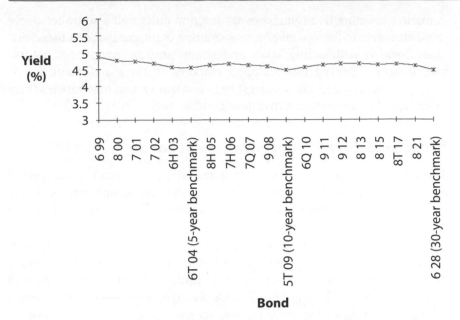

Figure 4.1 Gilt yield curve 23 June 2004,
showing 'expensive' benchmark bonds

Gilt	Yield	Gilt	Yield
6Q 04	4.87	5T 09 (10-year benchmark)	4.48
5 05	4.76	6Q 10	4.56
5Q 05	4.73	9 11	4.63
7H 06	4.67	9 12	4.66
6H 03	4.56	8 13	4.66
6T 04 (5-year benchmark)	4.55	8 15	4.63
8H 05	4.62	8T 17	4.65
7H 06	4.66	8 21	4.60
7Q 07	4.62	6 28 (30-year benchmark)	4.47
9 08	4.58		

market participants including market makers on issues such as what part of
the yield curve to tap for further borrowing, and the timing of auctions.
New instruments and structures are often introduced as a result of such
consultation, such as zero-coupon bonds (*strips*) and a repurchase facility.
Different classes of investors have an interest in different parts of the yield
curve, for example banks concentrate on the short end of the curve while
most fund managers will have more interest in the long end. The issuing
authorities usually attempt to meet the needs of all classes of investor.

A market structure that minimises transaction costs will also be relatively more attractive to foreign investors, so market participants recommend that taxes such as withholding taxes and stamp duty be removed. This has indeed been observed in developed markets. If taxes are retained it is usually in the government's interest to institute a system that enables them to be repaid to non-resident investors as soon as possible.

The secondary market in government bonds

The typical structure in government markets is for a group of designated banks and securities houses, registered with the central authority, to be the market makers or *primary dealers* in government bonds. These firms are required to maintain liquidity by making continuous two-way prices in all government bonds at all times that the market is open. They are usually also required to provide market intelligence to the issuing authority. In return for performing their market making function, primary dealers often are granted certain privileges, which usually include the right to participate at auctions, access to anonymous live-price dealing screens (usually as part of an *inter-dealer broker service*) and bond borrowing facilities at the issuing authority.

Although developed government markets frequently contain bonds of up to 30 years maturity, in emerging economies a market in short-dated securities develops before one in longer-dated bonds. This is why a *money market* in government Treasury bills often develops first.

In the descriptions that follow we introduce the main features of three euro area government markets and the US Treasury market.

GERMANY

Introduction

Although Germany no longer offers a deutschmark as the anchor currency for Europe, the German bond market is the continent's safe haven for global investors. This reflects the size and strength of the German economy and its superior performance in maintaining relatively stable inflation levels in the post-war period. Recently however with the introduction of the euro, the structures and institutions have been changing in Germany. For example although it built up a solid reputation in its handling of monetary policy and for keeping inflation at low levels, the Bundesbank lost much of its status with the introduction of the euro currency in 1999. Monetary policy is now the responsibility of the European Central Bank (ECB),

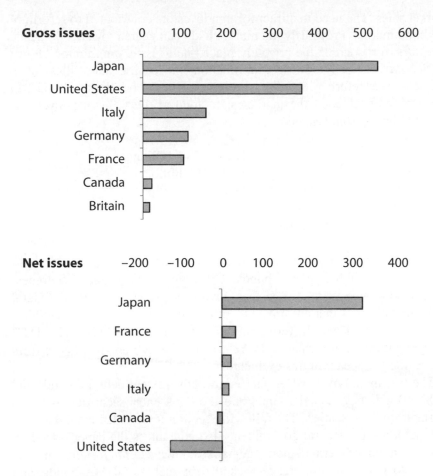

Figure 4.2 Selected government bond issuance in 2003, $billion
Source: Strata Consulting

which is based in Frankfurt. As such there is no longer the close scrutiny of the Bundesbank's repo rates and its open market operations that there once was. The Bundesbank targeted inflation mainly through controlling money supply, whereas the ECB does not have an explicit money supply target for the euro area.

Volumes and issuance

The rise in budget deficits through the 1990s resulted in Germany becoming a net importer of capital. Much of this was achieved through bond

market sales. The need to attract foreign investors contributed to reform of
the bond market. Previously the market had been geared towards domestic
investors, for example the privately placed notes issue programme known
as *Schuldscheine*. Following reunification, the central authorities introduced market reforms including the issue of liquid benchmark bonds. In
the beginning of 2003 the market size stood at the following levels, as
reported by the Bundesbank:

Bunds	DEM 373.5 billion
Bobls	DEM 195 billion
Schätze	DEM 72.3 billion
Federal savings bonds	DEM 67.4 billion
Treasury discount paper	DEM 19.2 billion

As well as federal government bonds, the German *Lander* and municipali-
ties also issue publicly placed bonds. These are more popular with domestic investors however, as overseas investors prefer to deal in federal
government bonds that are linked to futures contracts traded on London's
LIFFE and the Deutsch Termminbörse in Frankfurt (DTB). The DTB
merged with futures exchanges in Austria and Switzerland in 1999 to form
Eurex, the European futures exchange.

The two main types of German federal government debt are bunds and
Bobls. Bunds pay annual coupon and are book-entry securities listed on
German stock exchanges. The following section reviews the main features.

In addition the federal government also guarantees the paper issued by
the association of German mortgage banks known as *Pfandbriefe*, which is
similar to US agency mortgage-backed debt such as GNMA bonds, and
which enjoys a AAA rating. Information on the *Pfandbriefe* market can be
found at www.pfandbriefe.org

Market structure

German government bonds have been issued by the federal government as
well as public sector bodies such as the federal railway, the post office and
so on. The bund market is a large and liquid market, and essentially the
benchmark yield indicator for European government bonds. The most
common maturity for new bonds is 10 years.

The typical size of a new issue is €10–15 billion. Bonds of between
eight and 30 years maturity are normally issued. Seven days after issue the
bonds are listed, and trade on all eight of the domestic stock exchanges.
The Frankfurt bourse is the largest and most important exchange. Issue are

generally fixed coupon, bullet maturities. Trading is on a clean price basis. Banks and brokers quote prices on screens and these usually move in increments of €0.01. The typical transaction size is around €20 million, with price quotes of around €0.05 for liquid issues and €0.08–0.10 for less liquid issues.

New issue of stock takes place through a closed shop of banks and financial institutions, including foreign banks, known as the Federal Bond Syndicate (Konsortium). Around 100 firms make up this syndicate. Until 1990 the procedure for new issues was for all members of the consortium to be allocated a fixed percentage of the total issue size irrespective of the issue terms. From 1990 a new procedure was introduced, which involves splitting the issue into two tranches that combine the traditional method and a competitive auction. The first tranche has fixed terms, including issue price, and is allocated among syndicate members. The second tranche is auctioned, with bids made via consortium banks in €0.01 increments for bonds with the same conditions, except issue price, as the first tranche. Bids can be made until the morning after the launch date, and the Bundesbank allocates the stock within two hours after the auction close.

In the secondary market bunds settle via the domestic *Kassenverein* system, although investors who require custody outside of Germany can clear trades through Euroclear and Clearstream. Domestic settlement takes place two business days after trade date, although international settlement follows normal Eurobond practice and clears on T+3.

Interest on bunds is paid on an annual basis, and accrues from the previous coupon date (inclusive) to the settlement date (exclusive). The value date is always the same as the settlement date. There has been no provision for ex-dividend trading since 1994. Prior to the introduction of the euro at the start of 1999, bunds accrued interest on a 30/360 year day count basis. However in line with all euroland bonds they now accrue on an ACT/ACT basis. Yields can be calculated by any one of three methods, the ISMA method, Fangmeyer and Moosmuller. The differences between these methods are based on their assumptions about how to calculate the compound interest in a broken-year period. The ISMA method is used internationally. In the Fangmeyer and Moosmuller methods, simple interest is calculated for partial coupon periods while compound interest is calculated for full periods. The former calculation uses annual compounding while the latter compounds at the same frequency as coupon payments on the bond. So in fact for bunds the two methods produce identical yields.

Bundesobligationen (Bobls) are five-year federal notes. They were originally intended to promote the formation of financial capital by different social groups in the population. Foreign investors were permitted to purchase the notes after 1988. New issues range in size from DM500–10,000 million. They are vanilla bonds with fixed coupon and bullet payment on maturity. Like bunds a book-entry system is used and there are no physical bond certificates. Since 1995 the Bundesbank has held a quarterly auction of Bobls, and also discontinued issue of its four-year *Schätze* notes. In all other respects Bobls trade in a similar fashion to bunds.

ITALY

The size of the Italian public sector deficit, built up in the post-war period and extending into the 1970s and 1980s partly as a result of the country's large-scale subsidising of nationalised industries and generous social welfare system, has resulted in Italy having the world's third largest government bond market. Part of the economic criteria for countries planning to entering European monetary union (EMU) in 1999 was a commitment to stabilising and reducing public debt. The Italian government met the budget deficit criteria for EMU in part by levying a special one-off 'EMU tax'.[2] Nevertheless Italian government bonds should continue to play an important part in the global debt markets. Foreign investors held approximately 16 per cent of total Italian government debt at the beginning of 2001.[3]

The authorities have engaged on major reforms of the debt market over the last 15 years; the most notable was the separation of the central bank, the Bank of Italy, from the Treasury. A screen-based secondary market has also been introduced, as has the payment of gross coupons. The reforms were aimed at increasing the attractiveness of the government debt market for overseas investors. The Treasury also concentrated on a funding programme concentrated more on long-dated fixed-rate bonds, which are the instruments of greatest interest to foreign investors, and less on short-dated securities. The domestic investor base had traditionally been more attracted to short-dated instruments, a reflection of the inflation-prone Italian economy in the 1970s and 1980s. For example in 1981 over 66 per cent of the government borrowing requirement was met through the issue of short-term bonds known as 'BOTs', compared with 8 per cent of the debt raised through the long-dated bonds known as 'BTPs'. In 1994 the figures were 4 per cent and 77 per cent respectively, a significant turn-around. The longest-dated maturity was a 30-year bond. Nevertheless the average maturity of Italian government debt was three years in 2001, the lowest figure in Europe, although this was a higher figure than in 1982 when the average maturity was just one year.

Budget deficits are financed almost entirely through the public issue of securities. Roughly a quarter of the publicly placed debt is still comprised of *Buoni Ordinari del Tresoro* or BOTs. These are discount securities issued in three, six-, and 12-month maturity bands at fortnightly auctions. Unlike other European government markets there used to be virtually no demand for longer-dated paper, *Buoni del Tresoro Poliennali* or BTPs. This reflected the high-inflation economy that existed for many years. However these became more popular in the 1990s. BTPs originally paid a semi-annual coupon (although quoted as an annualised yield) but this was altered when markets were harmonised in preparation for EMU in 1999. The ten-year BTP contract on LIFFE was a major market instrument prior to EMU.

The other instruments introduced in an attempt to lengthen the average maturity of the debt stock were *Certificati di Credito del Tresoro* or CCTs, which are floating-rate notes first issued in 1977. Although longer-dated paper, they were linked to a moving index so therefore more attractive to domestic investors. Until 1994 CCTs paid a spread over the average yield of a range of BOT auctions; they also paid semi-annual coupons. Since 1995 CCT coupons are indexed to a single auction of the six-month BOT auction, subsequently changed to the 12-month BOT auction.

The newest instruments are the *Certificati del Tresoro a Zero Coupon* or CTZ, which are two-year zero-coupon notes and have been issued since 1995. These have proved popular with domestic retail investors. There is also a secondary market in *Certificati del Tresoro con Opzione* or CTOs, although these have not been issued since 1992 and account for only a small part of overall debt. They are similar to BTPs but contain an option which allows the bondholder to sell them back to the Treasury half-way through their nominal life.

Prior to introduction of the euro the Treasury, in line with other governments in the EU, issued ECU notes. These were known as *Certificati del Tresoro* in Ecu or CTEs. From 1993 the Treasury issued five-year CTEs, with fixed-rate annual coupon.

Market structure

The Italian government bond market is the third largest in the world, with nominal outstanding totalling L1723 trillion (US$996 billion) in January 1997. This debt is made up of the different bonds noted above. Roughly a third of the nominal outstanding are CCTs; another third is made up of fixed-rate BTPs. Government bonds are issued in book-entry form. However they can be converted into physical form on request. CTZs are available only in book-entry form.

All bonds trade on a clean price basis. Settlement is three business days after the trade date and clearing is available through Euroclear and Cedel. Government bonds used to pay interest on an annual and semi-annual basis, depending on the security, however all debt now pays an annual coupon. BTPs and CTOs, as well as CCTs with original maturities of seven years or less, originally paid coupons semi-annually, while all other types paid annually. Interest traditionally accrued from the previous coupon date (inclusive) to the settlement date (inclusive), so consequently the Italian accrual rules added one extra day of interest to comparable calculations in other markets. With the introduction of the single currency, however, this arrangement has been changed to bring it into line with other euro bond markets. In the same way the day count basis was changed from 30/360 to ACT/ACT as part of euro harmonisation. Bonds do not trade ex-dividend. ACT/365 is used for discounting.

Italian government bond yields are quoted gross of a withholding tax of 12.5 per cent, introduced in September 1987. There was a gap of six years before a procedure was introduced that enables foreign investors to claim reimbursement of this tax. The procedure itself was time-consuming and cumbersome. In 1994 a new computerised system was instituted which resulted in foreign investors receiving gross coupons promptly, and reimbursement of tax took 30 days. From June 1996 overseas bondholders received gross coupons, removing the issue of reimbursement completely.

Primary and secondary markets

The Bank of Italy advises the Treasury on funding issues and organises the auctions at which government bonds are sold. All new issue of paper is via an auction system, managed by the central bank. The Treasury announces annually the dates on which auctions will be held, and announces quarterly the bonds and minimum issue sizes that will be offered in the following three months. Auctions are held at the beginning and in the middle of the month. A new BTP series is normally issued every three months. A 'Dutch auction' system is used, which means that bonds are allotted to the highest bidders first, but all successful bidders pay the same price, known as the marginal price, which is that of the lowest accepted bid. The exception is for BOTs, which are US-style, with successful bidders paying the price at which they bid. The Treasury does not set a base price but it does calculate an exclusion price based on the average level of offers, in order to deter highly speculative or non-market bids. Auctions are automated using the national interbank network. Settlement takes place three business days after the auction date for all notes except BTPs and CCTs, which settle two days after the auction date. Secondary market settlement is on a T+3 basis.

From 1994 there has been a three-tier dealing system in the professional market. The primary dealers are known as government bond *specialists*, and are market makers in all issues. They must undertake to buy a minimum of 3 per cent of the nominal value of each auction. They are entitled to take up extra paper at the marginal price immediately after successful auctions. A curious arrangement in the Italian market is a second tier of market makers known as *primary dealers*, who have less onerous market-making responsibilities than specialists. The third tier of the structure is made up of ordinary dealers who fulfil a broker-dealer role. Specialists traded more than 60 per cent of cash market volume in 1996.

Market supervision is shared between the Treasury, the Bank of Italy and Consob, the stock exchange commission.

FRANCE

The French government bond market is one of the most liquid markets in the world. The central authorities have pursued a policy of targeting overseas investors, and the level of foreign holdings of French government debt rose from virtually nil in 1986 to over 35 per cent by 2001. This was achieved in part by following the US model of concentrating on large, liquid conventional bonds, and a regular pre-announced timetable of auctions of medium and long-dated bonds. France also introduced zero-coupon bonds in 1991, before either the UK or Germany. The French market is a transparent and efficient one, and an important part of the euro-denominated bonds market, although benchmark status in euro-government paper tends to be allocated to German government bonds.

The Treasury has simple issuance and settlement procedures which ensure high transparency and liquidity. The total nominal outstanding was €340.8 billion in December 2001. Of this about 63 per cent was made up of long-term debt, and the average maturity of total debt outstanding was 6½ years.

The primary market

The government's Ministry of the Economy is the central authority in government debt. The ministry has publicly stated its commitment to maintaining an orderly and transparent market that is keen to attract foreign investors. The market is made up three different instruments, which are:

Obligation Assimilable du Trésor (OATs), *Bons du Trésor à Taux Fixe et à Intérêt Annuel* (BTANs) and *Bons du Trésor à Taux Fixe et à Intérêt Précompté* (BTFs). OATs are the standard means of financing the central budget deficit; they are bonds with maturities of up to 30 years. BTANs are fixed-rate bonds of maturities of between two and five years, while BTFs are short-dated Treasury bills with a maximum maturity of one year. Like bills in other markets they are discount instruments. The Treasury issues one 13-week BTF each week, and alternately a six-month BTF and a one-year BTF.

Market liquidity is enhanced by a policy of issuing fungible debt, so that outstanding issues are frequently increased in size through regular issue of debt. Debt management is carried out through the *Fonds de Soutien des Rentes* or FSR, which is the government debt management fund.

Government auctions take place twice a month, with long-dated OATs auctioned on the first Thursday of each month and medium-term BTANs auctioned on the third Thursday. There is a weekly auction of BTFs every Monday, and every two months there is an additional issue of BTANs on the second Wednesday of the month. Details such as the security and amount of the auction are released two business days before the auction date. At the auction sealed bids may be handed in directly to the Bank of France, the central bank, although most market participants use a computerised remote bidding system known as Telsat. All bonds are listed on the Paris Stock Exchange, but trading also takes place in an active over-the-counter (OTC) market which is managed by primary dealers known as *Spécialistes en Valeurs du Trésor* or SVTs. The primary dealers are responsible for ensuring Treasury auctions are a success, and are required to make continuous prices in the secondary market. They account for almost 90 per cent of the securities sold at each auction. The auction system is on the US model, with highest bids being served first. Lower bids are served in quantities decided at the discretion of the Treasury. Auctions on the first Thursday of each month are for payment on the 25th or following business day. Bonds will trade in a grey market until this date, and SVTs quote two-way prices on a when issued basis up to one week before the auction date.

OATs are issued as existing tranches of existing bonds, so that the current size of some OATs is as large as €16 billion. The Treasury announces an issuance calendar at the start of each year. Typically the 10-year bond as well as the long bond (30-year) are reopened every month. Bonds are issued in book-entry form so physical paper is unavailable. Most OATs are fixed coupon bonds with bullet maturities, paying interest on an annual basis. There are some esoteric older issues in existence, however, with special features. For example the variable rate January 2004 issue is based on the average yield of long-term government bonds over the 12-month period preceding the coupon payment.

BTANs are fixed interest Treasury notes with maturities of up to five years. They are the main instrument the Treasury uses for short-term government financing, together with bills (BTFs). There is little distinction in the secondary market however, where BTANs trade like medium-dated OATs. The paper is issued in book-entry form without certificates. The Treasury uses a fungible issuance procedure for BTANs; two-year and five-year notes are issued every month. Like OATs the paper is traded in the OTC market, which is managed by the SVTs. The key difference between the two types of bonds is in the basis of trading: BTANs trade on a yield basis, with annualised yields quoted to three decimal places. The bid–offer spread is around 2 basis points on average. In most other respects the bonds have similar terms and arrangements to OATs.

The secondary market

OATs are tradable on the Paris stock exchange but the majority of market dealing is on an OTC basis. There is a screen-based price system for OATs, with the bid-offer spread generally around 5–15 centimes for liquid issues. Prices are quoted net of tax and costs. OATs trade on a clean price basis. Coupon is paid gross to non-residents.

Clearing takes place three days after trade date for domestic and international settlement. Bonds are cleared internationally through Euroclear and Cedel or domestically through the Paris stock exchange clearing system, known as SICOVAM. Settlement takes place on T+1 or T+3 for bonds traded domestically and on T+3 for international trades. Transactions between primary market dealers take place on a delivery versus payment basis.

French government bond futures are traded on the *Marché à Terme International de France,* or MATIF, which was founded in 1986 and is one of the largest futures and options exchanges in the euro area. Prior to EMU its key contracts were the futures and options on a notional 7-to-10 year French government bond known as the 'notionnel'. It now trades futures and options on a notional 10-year euro-denominated bond.

BTANs and BTFs are only tradeable on an OTC basis. The SVTs announce bid and offer prices together with the volume available for trading at those prices. BTANs are quoted on a yield basis and the rate of return is expressed as an annualised rate over 365 days, while BTFs are quoted on a money market straight-line yield expressed as an annual percentage over 360 days. BTANs and BTFs are delivered and settled through the 'Saturne' system run by the Bank of France. The market is very liquid and transparent;

BTANs are among the most liquid short-term securities in Europe. There is a large and liquid repurchase (repo) market in government securities; unusually repo market makers are registered at the Bank of France.

French government bonds have a slightly unusual arrangement for the calculation of accrued interest, which depends on the type of settlement. Bonds settled T+3 in the domestic market via SICOVAM accrue from the previous coupon date (inclusive) to the trade date (exclusive). All other domestic settlement and international settlement results in accrual from the previous coupon date (inclusive) to the settlement date (exclusive). There is no facility for ex-dividend trading in OATs. The day count basis has always been ACT/ACT in the French market, which mean that no adjustment was necessary after the introduction of the euro.

OAT strips

After the US market, the French government market was one of the first to introduce zero-coupon bonds or strips. Subsequently both Belgium and the Netherlands introduced strips. In France the Treasury has allowed primary dealers to strip long-dated OATs since June 1991. The range of bonds that may be stripped has been more restricted than in the US market, but all but two of the 10-year and longer-dated OATs are now strippable. Essentially all OATs maturing on 25 April and 25 October may be stripped. The first bond to be designated was the 30-year bond, the 8.5% 2019. The mechanics of the stripping process are:

■ All SVTs are allowed to strip and reconstitute bonds eligible for stripping. The minimum amount to be stripped was FF20 million (pre-euro).
■ Stripping and reconstitution is carried out via SICOVAM, and is free of charge.

As at November 2002, 22 bonds could be stripped.

EURO-ZONE INFORMATION SOURCES

Outside of the local market area the best information source for private investors remains the *Financial Times*. The Bloomberg website www.bloomberg.com and www.bloomberg.co.uk also report bond prices, yields and yield curves. The investment bank Barclays Capital also carries information on euro government bonds on its website, www.barclays capital.com.

THE US TREASURY MARKET

Introduction

The US Treasury marker is the largest bond market in the world and unsurprisingly, given the importance of the US economy in the world, the most important in macroeconomic terms. It is also reasonably accessible to investors outside the USA. For example, private investors can open a US dollar account with a stockbroker such as Charles Schwab or CSFBDirect, over the telephone or the Internet, and buy and sell US Treasury securities. Treasury securities are the benchmark for the rest of the global debt capital markets, with the spread over the Treasury being the indicator of any obligor's creditworthiness.

Treasuries are issued by the US Federal Reserve (Fed) via an auction system. There are three types of securities issued, which are:

- bills, which are discount instruments of between one month and one year maturity
- notes, which are bonds of between 1 and 10 years
- bonds, which are bonds of between 10 and 30 years maturity (in fact the Fed announced the discontinuance of its 30-year bond, because of a reduction in the size of budget deficits, then in January 2006 issued a 30-year for the first time in four years).

There is no real difference between notes and bonds, they are both vanilla bonds. They are semi-annual coupon bonds, like gilts, and are also still quoted in 'ticks' or 32nds. One tick is therefore 0.01325. If a Treasury price is given as 99-16 it means 99 and 16/32 or 99.50.[4]

Treasury dealing by private investors

As we noted above, it is fairly easy for private investors to deal in Treasuries, for instance via an Internet online brokerage service. Non-US residents will generally have to open an account and wire US dollars across to their account. They will also need to complete a non-resident tax declaration, in order to receive coupon gross of tax. A local custody service will hold the bonds on behalf of non-resident investors. The Fed operates its own service for private investors, known as Treasury Direct. The Fed's website www.federal reserve.gov carries a wealth of information on the Treasury market.

Outside the USA a good source of information on Treasuries is the *Wall Street Journal*. The Bloomberg website also carries information on the market. Another useful information source is the US Bureau of Public Debt, which also has a direct dealing service for US residents. Its website is www.publicdebt.treas.gov. Finally the website www.longbond.com will be of use to Treasury investors.

Notes

1 Including, I am unashamed to say, myself!
2 The criteria for countries entering EMU included a budget deficit no larger than 3 per cent of GDP and gross public debt no larger than 60 per cent of GDP. However certain criteria were relaxed, for example the Italian and Belgian gross public debt levels were at over 100 per cent of GDP at the time of entry to EMU.
3 Source: Banca d'Italia.
4 Gilts also used to be priced in ticks but alas, converted to decimal pricing in 1998.

CHAPTER 5

Corporate bonds, Eurobonds and credit quality

The bonds we have talked about up to now have all been fairly high quality. For instance, gilts are AAA-rated and absolutely safe. They are safer than a bank account and if you hold them to maturity you will always get your money back. There are a large number of other bonds that are not absolutely safe, however, issued by lower-rated governments and by corporates.

Private investors should be fully aware of the risks they are taking on whenever they invest in corporate bonds. It is important to remember that the risks in holding a bond are asymmetric. This means that the downside is greater than the upside. The upside is known pretty much with certainty: receipt of coupons and then repayment of initial investment. It is possible to make substantial capital gains from investing in bonds, even with government bonds. If you buy a bond that has been issued at a time of high interest rates, you can realise high capital gains as interest rates fall. But this should be seen as a bonus. On the other hand, the downside is potentially very high: practically the entire investment. This will happen if the issuer defaults. With corporate bonds, this remains a possibility.

For this reason, you should exercise a little more care when evaluating corporate bonds. You should consider the formal credit rating assigned to the bond, by one or more of the ratings agencies. You may also wish to use your own assessment of the name, for example when considering the bonds of well-known companies. This name recognition can be higher than the formal rating. For instance, you might be (as the author is) quite happy to hold bonds issued by UK building societies, despite their having lower than the AAA rating. This is because you might be very familiar with the name and reasonably confident that the organisation will not default.

In this chapter I describe corporate bonds and international bonds issued by corporates (as well as governments), known as Eurobonds. We shall also look at credit ratings.

CORPORATE BONDS

The corporate markets cover a wide range of instruments and issuer currencies. There is a great variety of structures and products traded in the corporate markets. All instruments serve the same primary purpose, however, of serving as an instrument of corporate finance. The exotic structures that exist have usually been introduced in order to attract new investors, or retain existing investors, in what is an extremely competitive market.

Generally the term 'corporate markets' is used to cover bonds issued by non-government borrowers. The bonds issued by regional governments and certain public sector bodies, such as national power and telecommunications utilities, are usually included as 'government' debt, as they almost always are covered by an explicit or implicit government guarantee. All other categories of borrower are therefore deemed to be 'corporate' borrowers. The combined market is a large one, as was indicated in the previous chapter. Table 5.1 shows non-government international bond issuance from 2001, split by currency. The majority of bonds are denominated in US dollars, euros and Japanese yen.

The euro, introduced in 11 countries of the EU in January 1999, has not unexpectedly become a popular currency for corporate bond issuers. Corporate bond issues in sterling are detailed in Figure 5.1, split into maturity bands of short, medium and long-dated bond issues.

Introduction

Corporate bonds are tradable debt instruments issued by non-government borrowers. The majority of corporate bonds are plain vanilla instruments, paying a fixed coupon and with a fixed term to maturity. Corporate

TABLE 5.1 Non-government international bond issuance					
	US$	**Sterling**	**Euro**	**Other**	**Total**
2001	261	51	153	108	573
2002	334	63	148	86	631
2003	342	78	209	65	693
2004	381	102	332	88	903

Volumes are US$ billion
Source: CapitalData Bondware; Bank of England.

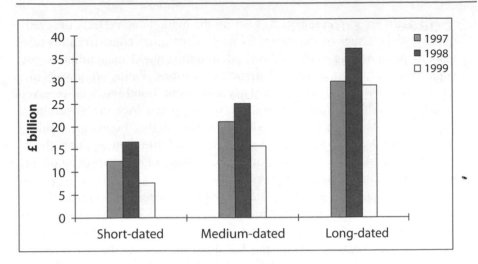

Figure 5.1 Sterling non-government bond issuance

Source: BoE

issuers use the debt capital markets to raise finance for short, medium and long-term requirements and projects. Corporate borrowers raise both *secured* and *unsecured debt*, with the former type of borrowing secured on assets of the company. The ease with which a corporation can raise unsecured finance in the public market is a function of its *credit rating*. Often corporate bonds are classified by the type of issuer, for example banks and financial services companies, utility companies and so on. Issuer classification is then broken down further, for example utility companies are subdivided into electricity companies, water companies and gas distribution companies.

Under the terms of any corporate bond issue, the borrower is obliged to pay the periodic interest on the loan, represented by the coupon rate, as well as repay the principal on maturity of the debt. If the borrower fails to pay interest on the loan as it is due, or to repay the principal on maturity, this is known as *default* and the borrower will be in breach of the terms of the issue.[1] This is a serious event. In the event of default bondholders are entitled to enforce payment via the legal process and the courts. As providers of debt finance, bondholders rank higher than preferred and ordinary shareholders in the event of a wind-up of the company. Depending on the level of the *security* associated with the particular bond issue, bondholders may rank ahead of other creditors. The issue of the *credit risk* of a specific issuer is the key concern for corporate bond investors.

The yield on corporate bonds is set by the market and reflects the credit quality of the issuer of the paper, as well as the other considerations relevant to price setting such as level of liquidity, yield on similar bonds, supply and demand and general market conditions. Yields are always at a *spread* above the similar maturity government bond. A well-received corporate bond will trade at a relatively low spread over the government yield curve. Although the common perception is that bonds are held by investors for their income, and are less price volatile than equities, this is an over-generalisation. Certain bonds are highly volatile, while others are held for their anticipated price appreciation.

Certain corporate issues are aimed at only the professional (institutional) market and have minimum denominations of US$10,000 or £10,000. Generally however they are issued in denominations of US$1,000 (or £1,000, €1,000 and so on). In the US domestic market the par value for corporate bonds is sometimes taken to be US$1,000 instead of the more conventional US$100. A market order to purchase '100 bonds' (or simply '100') would therefore mean $100,000 nominal of the bond. In other markets, though, the standard convention is followed of using 100 as the par value of the bond.

Basic provisions

The majority of corporate bonds are term bonds: that is, they will have a fixed term to maturity, at which point they must be redeemed by the borrower. Only companies of the highest quality can issue bonds of maturity much greater than 10 years at anything less than prohibitive cost; however it is common to see long-dated bonds of up to 30 years maturity or longer issued by high credit-quality companies. Let us look at some other relevant features.

Bond security

A corporate that is seeking lower-cost debt, or that does not have a sufficiently high credit rating, may issue secured debt. As security the issuer will pledge either fixed assets such as land and buildings, or personal property. The security offered may be fixed, in which case a specific asset is tied to the loan, or *floating*, meaning that the general assets of the company are offered as security for the loan, but not any specific asset. A *mortgage debenture* gives bondholders a charge over the pledged assets, called a *lien* (a lien is a legal right to sell mortgaged property to satisfy unpaid obligations to creditors). Where companies do not own fixed assets or other real property they often offer as collateral securities of other companies that they hold. A *debenture* bond is not secured by a specific pledge of property, but bondholders have a claim over company assets in general, often ahead of other creditors.

Provisions for paying off bonds

In some cases a corporate issue will have a call provision, which gives the issuer the option to buy back all or part of the issue before maturity. The issuer will find a call option useful as it means that debt can be refinanced when market interest rates drop below the rate currently being paid, without having to wait until the bond's maturity. At the same time such a provision is disadvantageous to the bondholder, who will require a higher yield as compensation.

Call provisions can take various forms. There may be a requirement for the issuer to redeem a pre-determined amount of the issue at regular intervals. Such a provision is known as a *sinking fund* requirement. This type of provision for repayment of corporate debt may be designed to retire all of a bond issue by the maturity date, or it may be arranged to pay off only a part of the total by the end of the term. If only a part is paid off, the remaining balance is known as a *balloon maturity*. The purpose of a sinking fund is to reduce the credit risk attached to the bond. Investors will derive comfort from the fact that provisions have been made regarding the final redemption of the bond, and will be more willing to buy the bond. Clearly this may be necessary for borrowers of lower credit quality.

In most cases the issuer will satisfy any sinking fund requirement by either making a cash payment of the face amount of the bonds to be redeemed to the bond trustee, who will call the bonds for repayment by drawing serial numbers randomly, or by delivering to the trustee bonds with a total face value equal to the amount that must be retired from bonds purchased in the open market. The sinking fund call price, as with callable bonds generally, is the par value of the bonds, although in a few cases there may be a set percentage of par that is redeemable.

The primary market

The issue of corporate debt in the capital markets require a primary market mechanism. The first requirement is a collection of merchant banks or investment banks that possess the necessary expertise. Investment banks provide advisory services on corporate finance as well as *underwriting* services, which give a guarantee to place an entire bond issue into the market in return for a fee.[2] As part of the underwriting process the invest-ment bank will either guarantee a minimum price for the bonds, or aim to place the paper at the best price available.

Small-sized bond issues may be underwritten by a single bank. It is common however for larger issues, or issues that are aimed at a cross-border investor base, to be underwritten by a *syndicate* of investment banks. This is a group of banks that collectively underwrite a bond issue, with each syndicate member being responsible for placing a proportion of the issue. The bank that originally won the *mandate* to place the paper invites other banks to join the syndicate. This bank is known as the *lead underwriter, lead manager* or *book-runner.* An issue is brought to the market simultaneously by all syndicate members, usually via the *fixed price re-offer* mechanism. This is designed to guard against some syndicate members in an offering selling stock at a discount in the grey market, to attract investors, which would force the lead manager to buy the bonds back if it wished to support the price. Under the fixed price re-offer method, price undercutting is not possible as all banks are obliged not to sell their bonds below the initial offer price that has been set for the issue. The fixed price is usually in place up to the first settlement date, after which the bond is free to trade in the secondary market.

A corporate debt issue is priced over the same yield curve as a government bond. The extent of a corporate bond's yield spread over the government yield curve is a function of the market's view of the credit risk of the issuer (for which formal credit ratings are usually used) and the perception of the liquidity of the issue. The pricing of corporate bonds is sometimes expressed as a spread over the equivalent maturity government bond, rather than as an explicit stated yield, or sometimes as a spread over another market reference index such as LIBOR. If there is no government bond of the same maturity as the corporate bond, the issuing bank will price the bond over an interpo-lated yield, obtained from the yields of two government bonds with maturi-ties lying either side of the corporate issue. If there is no government bond that has a maturity beyond the corporate issue, the practice in developed economies is to take a spread over the longest-dated government issue. In developing markets, however, the bond would probably not be issued.

Formal credit ratings are important in the corporate markets. Investors usually use a domestic rating agency in conjunction with the established international agency: Moody's, Standard & Poors or FitchIBCA. As formal ratings are viewed as important by investors, it is in the interest of issuing companies to seek a rating from an established agency, especially if they are seeking to issue foreign currency and/or place their debt across national boundaries.

The secondary market

Corporate bonds virtually everywhere are traded on an over-the-counter (OTC) basis, that is, directly between counterparties over the telephone. Bonds are usually nevertheless listed on an exchange though, as many institutional investors have limitations on the extent to which they may hold non-listed instruments. Eurobonds for example are usually listed on the London Stock Exchange or Luxembourg Stock Exchange, while those issued by Asian borrowers are frequently also listed on the Hong Kong or Singapore exchanges. In the USA there are more corporate bond issues listed on the New York Stock Exchange (NYSE) than there are equities, and the dollar value of daily bond trading is at least as high as that in equities. On the NYSE a low volume of trading in bonds does take place on the exchange itself, but this dwarfed by the volume of trading in the OTC market.

The level of liquidity varies greatly for corporate bonds, ranging from completely liquid (for example, a World Bank global bond issue) to completely illiquid, which is common when investors have bought the entire issue of a bond and hold it to maturity. The number of market makers in a particular issue will also determine its liquidity. In return for providing liquidity, market makers also retain a major market privilege because they have exclusive access to inter-dealer broker price screens.

Another factor that is important to secondary market liquidity is the clearance and settlement system. In Japan for example, the settlement system until very recently was a decentralised, paper-based system, which acted as a barrier to market liquidity. A computerised, dematerialised 'book-entry' system for settling corporate bonds, as represented by Euroclear and Clearstream, contributes to liquidity because it assists market participants to trade without being exposed to delivery or payment risk.

Fundamentals of corporate bonds

The market generally classifies corporate bonds by credit rating and by sector of issuer. In the USA for example issuers are classified as public utilities, transport companies, industrial companies, banking and financial institutions, and international (or Yankee) borrowers. Within these broad categories issuers are broken down further, for example transportation companies are segmented into airlines, railway companies and road transport companies. In other respects corporate bonds have similar characteristics to those described in Chapter 1, although it is often in the corporate market that exotic or engineered instruments are encountered, compared with the generally plain vanilla government market.

Term to maturity

In the corporate markets, bond issues usually have a stated term to maturity, although the term is often not fixed because of the addition of call or put features. The convention is for most corporate issues to be medium or long-dated, and rarely to have a term greater than 20 years. In the US market prior to the Second World War it was common for companies to issue bonds with maturities of 100 years or more, but this is now quite rare. Only the highest-rated companies find it possible to issue bonds with terms to maturity greater than 30 years; during the 1990s such companies included Coca-Cola, Disney and British Gas.

Investors prefer to hold bonds with relatively short maturities because of the greater price volatility experienced in the markets since the 1970s, when high inflation and high interest rates were common. A shorter-dated bond has lower interest rate risk and price volatility than a longer-dated bond. There is thus a conflict between investors, whose wish is to hold bonds of shorter maturities, and borrowers, who would like to fix their borrowing for as long a period as possible. Although certain institutional investors such as pension fund managers have an interest in holding 30-year bonds, it would be difficult for all but the largest, best-rated companies to issue debt with a maturity greater than this.

Bond interest payment

Corporate bonds pay a fixed or floating-rate coupon. Floating-rate bonds were introduced in Chapter 2. Zero-coupon bonds are also popular in the corporate market, indeed corporate zero-coupon bonds differ from zero-coupon bonds in government markets in that they are actually issued by the borrower, rather than simply being the result of a market maker stripping a conventional coupon bond, as happens in government strip markets.

The fixed interest rate payable by a conventional bond is called the bond *coupon,* and we used this term when describing bonds in Chapter 1. The term originates from the time when bonds were bearer instruments, and were issued with coupons attached to them. The bondholder would tear off each coupon and post it to the issuer as each interest payment became due. These days bonds are *registered* instruments, and the investor receives the interest payment automatically from the issuer's registrar or paying agent. Therefore it is technically incorrect to refer to a bond's 'coupon' but the convention persists from earlier market infrastructure.[3] Many bond issues including Eurobonds and US Treasuries are held in 'dematerialised' form, which means only one 'global' certificate is issued, which is held with the clearing or custody agent, and investors receive a computer print-out detailing their bond holding.

Zero-coupon bonds are issued in their own right in the corporate markets, but are otherwise similar to zero-coupon bonds in government markets. Note that the term 'strip' for a zero-coupon bond is usually used only in the context of a government bond strip. In the US market zero-coupon bonds or 'zeros' were first issued in 1981 and initially offered tax advantages for investors, who avoided the income tax charge associated with coupon bonds.[4] However the tax authorities in the USA implemented legislation that treated the capital gain on zeros as income, thus wiping out the tax advantage. The tax treatment for zeros is similar in most jurisdictions. Zeros are still popular with investors, however, because they carry no reinvestment risk. The lack of reinvestment risk is appreciated more by investors in a declining interest rate environment, whereas in a rising interest rate environment investors may prefer to have coupon to reinvest. Zeros are also preferred during a period of relatively high interest rates, as the compounding effect is greater.

Bond security

International bonds and bonds sold in the Euro markets are unsecured. It is sometimes said that the best type of security is a company in sound financial shape that is able to service its debt out of its general cash flow, or a company with a high credit rating. While this is undoubtedly true, a secured bond is sometimes preferred by investors. In domestic markets, corporate bonds are often issued with a form of security attached in order to make them more palatable to investors. The type of security that is offered varies, and can be either *fixed* or *floating*, that is, a specific or general charge respectively on the assets of the borrowing company. The type of security sometimes defines the market that the bond trades in, for example a mortgage-backed bond or a debenture.

Call and refund provisions

A large number of corporate bonds, especially in the US market, have a call provision ahead of the stated maturity date. Borrowers prefer to have this provision attached to their bonds as it enables them to refinance debt at cheaper rates when market interest rates have fallen significantly below the level they were at the time of the bond issue. A call provision is a negative feature for investors, as bonds are only paid off if their price has risen above par. Although a call feature indicates an issuer's interest in paying off the bond, because they are not attractive for investors, callable bonds pay a higher yield than non-callable bonds of the same credit quality.

In general callable bonds are not callable for the first five or 10 years of their life, a feature that grants an element of protection for investors. Thereafter a bond is usually callable on set dates up to the final maturity date. In the US market another restriction is created by *refunding redemption*. This prohibits repayment of bonds within a set period after issue with funds obtained at a lower interest rate or through issue of bonds that rank with or ahead of the bond being redeemed. A bond with refunding protection during the first five or 10 years of its life is not as attractive as a bond with absolute call protection. Bonds that are called are usually called at par, although it is common also for bonds to have a call schedule that states that they are redeemable at specified prices above par during the call period.

There are also bonds that are callable only in part rather than in whole. In this case the issuer or trustee will select the bonds to be repaid on a random basis, with the serial numbers of the bonds being called published in major news publications.

PIBS: A STERLING INVESTOR'S FAVOURITE[5]

It is worth saying a few words about PIBS. This stands for **p**ermanent **i**nterest-**b**earing **s**hares, and refers to a class of undated bonds issued by UK building societies, so it is a type of bond peculiar to the sterling market in London. Most of them have very high coupons because they were issued in the early 1990s when sterling interest rates were comparatively high. As interest rates fell the prices of these bonds rose to very high levels, sometimes over 200 per cent. The high coupon on these bonds reflects the formal credit rating of building societies. However in the history of the building society there has never been a default or bankruptcy, so the high coupon represents very good value. It is also of value to investors who seek income.

Here's what I said in an account of PIBS in another book (*The Bond and Money Markets: Strategy, Trading, Analysis* (2001)):

> PIBS are very similar to preference shares issued by banks. That is, they are irredeemable (like preference shares and ordinary shares) and they are loss-absorbing, again like preference and ordinary shares, in that a building society can elect not to pay the coupon (dividend) due on PIBS if doing so would leave the society insolvent. PIBS are very attractive to societies and can therefore be issued at

higher margins over gilts than bank preference shares and still appear relatively cheap to the issuer.

The first issue of PIBS was in 1991 when Hoare Govett Securities Limited raised £75 million for Leeds Permanent Building Society (subsequently merged with and now part of Halifax plc). Further developments included the introduction of floating rate PIBS. Issuing such paper resulted in the building societies involved being rated for the first time. The highest-rated societies such as Halifax and Cheltenham & Gloucester subsequently either converted into banks, with shares listed on the London Stock Exchange, or were taken over by banks.

In theory PIBS offer no certainty that the capital is secure, because the issuing building society is under no obligation to repay the principal. However no building society has ever gone out of business in the history of the movement (the oldest building society currently still in existence, the Chesham BS, dates from 1845); where individual societies have found themselves in difficulties in the past, they have been taken over by another society. PIBS have delivered significant increases in capital gain for their holders, as sterling interest rates have fallen greatly from the levels that existed at the time most of the bonds were issued. They continue to trade in a liquid market.

The building society movement has contracted somewhat in recent years, as the largest societies converted to banks or were taken over by banking groups.[6] This resulted in the PIBS sector experiencing a decline in recent years as no new issues were placed in the market. In October 1999 Manchester Building Society issued £5 million nominal of paper, this being the first new issue of PIBS since 1993. The bonds were placed by Barclays Capital, and the small size of the issue indicates that the paper was aimed largely at retail customers rather than institutions. The bonds had a coupon of 8 per cent and were priced over the long-dated UK gilt, the 6% 2028.

Figure 5.2 shows PIBS in the market as at 10 December 2005.

CORPORATE BOND RISKS

The risks associated with holding corporate bonds include the interest rate risk we discussed in Chapter 2. Corporate bonds hold additional risk for investors, in the form of credit risk.

Permanent interest-bearing shares

FIXED RATE	%Gross Coupon	Buying price	%Gross yield	Issue price	Minimum purchase
Britannia	13.000	220.00	5.91	100.43	1,000
Cheshire	6.875	117.00	5.88	98.82	1,000
Coventry	12.125	205.00	5.91	100.75	1,000
Leeds Building Society	13.375	225.00	5.94	100.23	1,000
Manchester	8.000	141.00	5.67	100.00	1,000
Newcastle	10.750	186.00	5.78	100.32	1,000
Newcastle	12.625	216.00	5.84	100.32	1,000
Nottingham	7.875	135.00	5.83	98.00	5,000
Portman	6.250	111.00	5.63	100.00	1,000
Portman	7.250	118.00	6.14	100.00	1,000
Scarborough	8.500	151.00	5.63	100.00	2,500
Skipton	12.875	221.00	5.83	100.48	1,000
PERPETUAL SUBORDINATED BONDS					
Bradford & Bingley	11.625	194.00	5.99	100.13	10,000
Bradford & Bingley	13.000	217.00	5.99	100.20	10,000
Bristol & West	13.375	224.00	5.97	100.34	1,000
Cheltenham & Gloucester	11.750	198.00	5.93	100.98	50,000
First Active	11.750	194.00	6.00	100.25	10,000
Halifax	8.750	135.00	6.48	100.62	50,000
Halifax	9.375	163.00	5.75	100.17	1,000
Halifax	12.000	167.00	7.19	100.28	50,000
Halifax	13.625	231.00	5.90	100.00	50,000
Northern Rock	12.625	220.00	5.74	100.48	1,000

Figure 5.2 PIBS and perpetual subordinated bonds of building societies and former building societies as at December 2005

Source: extract from *The Times*, 10 December 2005. © News International. Reproduced with permission.

Credit risk

Unlike a (developed economy) government bond, holding a corporate bond exposes investors to *credit risk*, also known as *default risk*. This is the risk that the issuing company will default on its bond's coupon payments or principal repayment, resulting in a loss to the bondholders. Default may occur as a result of general financial difficulties, which might turn out to be short-term in nature, or to be a prelude to bankruptcy and liquidation. In the most extreme case it may be many years, if ever, before investors receive some of their money back.

The price of a corporate bond reflects the market's view of the credit risk associated with holding it. If the credit risk is perceived to be low, the spread of the issuer's bonds over the equivalent-maturity government bond will be low, while if the credit risk is deemed to be high, the yield spread will be correspondingly higher. This yield spread is sometimes referred to as the *credit spread* or *quality spread*. A 10-year bond issued by a highly rated corporate borrower will have a lower spread than a 10-year bond issued by a borrower with a lower credit rating. The higher yield on the bond issued by the lower-rated borrower is the compensation required by investors for holding the paper. Bond issuers are rated for their credit risk by both investment houses' internal credit analysts and formal rating agencies such as Standard & Poors, Moody's, and Fitch.

Figure 5.3 illustrates a hypothetical 'credit structure of interest rates'. The credit structure is dynamic and will fluctuate with changes in market conditions and the general health of the economy.

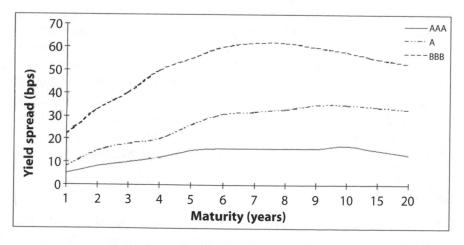

Figure 5.3 Credit structure of interest rates

Credit spreads over government yields and between corporate borrowers of different credit quality fluctuate with market conditions and in line with the business cycle. Spreads are highest when a country is in a recession and corporate health is relatively weak. A significant downward market correction also tends to widen credit spreads, as investors embark on a 'flight to quality' that depresses government bond yields. At the height of an economic boom spreads tend to be at their narrowest, not only because corporate balance sheets are in healthy shape but also because investors become less risk averse in times of a strong economy. This affects low-rated borrowers as well as highly-rated ones, so that spreads fall generally during an economic boom. In Figure 5.3 note how the credit spread for the hypothetical BBB-rated bonds falls as maturity increases; this is because analysts view the credit spread as being more liable to improve over time, as a company is upgraded, while a bond issued by a company that is already well rated can only stay where it is or suffer a downgrade.

Liquidity risk

A bond with a ready market of buyers and sellers is always more attractive to investors than one that is difficult to trade. Such a bond is called a *liquid* bond. *Liquidity* is a function of the ease with which market participants may buy or sell a particular bond, the number of market makers that are prepared to quote prices for the bond, and the spread between the buying and selling price (the bid offer spread). Illiquid bonds will have wide spreads and perhaps a lack of market makers willing to quote a bid price for them. Although some government bonds can sometimes be illiquid, liquidity risk, which is the risk that a bond held by an investor becomes illiquid, is a primarily a corporate bond market risk. The yield on a bond that is, or about to become, illiquid will be marked up by the market in compensation for the added risk of holding it. The best gauge of an issues liquidity is the size of its bid–offer spread. Government bonds frequently have a spread of 0.03 per cent or less, which is considered very liquid. Corporate spreads are wider but a spread of 0.10 to 0.25, up to 0.50 or 1 per cent is considered liquid. A bid–offer spread wider than this is considered illiquid, while a spread of say 1 per cent or more is virtually non-tradable. Some bonds are not quoted with a bid price or an offer price, indicating they are completely illiquid.

Call risk

In the previous section we stated that many domestic bond issues in the US market have call or refunding features attached to them. Such callable bonds have an added risk associated with holding them, known as *call risk*. This is the risk that the bond will be called at a time and price that is disadvantageous to bondholders or exposes them to loss. For example consider a 10-year bond with a call provision that states that the bond may be called at any time after the first five years, at par. For the last five years of the bond's life, when market interest rates fall below the bond's coupon rate, the price of the bond will not rise above par by as much as that of a similar maturity (and similar credit quality) bond that has no call feature. The price/yield relationship of a bond callable at par differs from a conventional bond, as the price will be less responsive to downward moves in yield once the price is at par.

Event risk

Event risk is peculiar to corporate bonds. This is the risk that, as a result of an unexpected corporate event, the credit risk of a bond increases greatly, so that the yield of the bond rises very quickly to much higher levels. The events can be external to the company, such as a natural disaster or regulatory change, or internal such as a merger or acquisition. A natural disaster may be an earthquake or flood, while regulatory change might be a change in the accounting or tax treatment of certain types of corporate debt.

Event risk can affect companies across an industry. An example of this was the fall of Barings Bank in 1995. The owners of Barings subordinated perpetual bonds suffered a loss as a result of the bankruptcy of the company. Holders of bonds issued by similar companies also suffered losses, as the market marked up the yields on these bonds as well. Figure 5.4 shows the change in average yield spread for bonds issued by N.M. Rothschild and Robert Fleming at the time of the Barings crash.

A takeover is another example of an event that may result in loss for bondholders. For example if as a result of a merger or takeover the debt of the amalgamated company is downgraded, bondholders will suffer a loss in capital value.

To protect against event risk, bonds may have provisions in them that require an acquiring company to repurchase them, under specified conditions. Such provisions are known as *poison puts*. Other features that may be included in the terms of corporate bonds are *maintenance of net worth* and *offer to redeem* clauses. The former provision states that if an issue falls below a certain level of net worth, the borrower must redeem the bond at par. The latter clause is similar except that it does not apply to an entire issue, but only to those bonds whose holders wish to redeem.

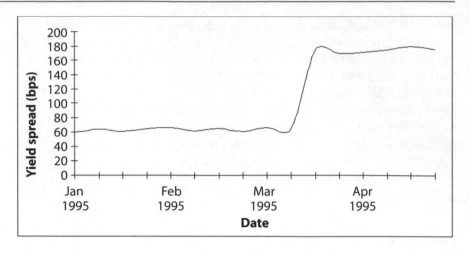

Figure 5.4 Impact of Barings Bank crisis on yield spreads
of bonds issued by similar companies

HIGH YIELD CORPORATE BONDS

High yield bonds were developed in the US corporate bond market, and have
not as yet emerged as a significant investment outside the dollar market,
except perhaps in the UK. They are also known as *junk bonds*, and this term
is still used. They refer to bond issues with very low credit ratings, below
BBB or Baa3. Bonds in this category may not necessarily have started life as
high-yield debt; they may have been rated as investment grade when originally issued and then suffered successive rating downgrades until rated as
non-investment grade. The majority of high-yield bonds however were rated
as below investment grade at the time of issue. Some of the bond structures
are quite sophisticated examples of financial engineering. For example a
high-yield bond structure may include deferred coupons, with no coupon
payments for a number of years after issue. This recognises the fact that the
debt burden of the issuer may result in severe cash flow problems in the early
years, so that coupons are deferred. Where there is a deferred coupon structure, the bond may include a *step-up* feature, so that after a period of time the
coupon rate is increased, to compensate for the low (or zero) coupon rate at
the start of the bond's life.

The author has four more words to say to private investors who may be
thinking of buying high yield bonds.

Do not buy them.

EUROBONDS

Nowhere has the increasing integration and globalisation of the world's capital markets been more evident than in the Eurobond market. It is an important source of funds for many banks and corporates, not to mention central governments. The key feature of Eurobonds is the way they are issued, internationally across borders and by an international underwriting syndicate. The method of issuing Eurobonds reflects the cross-border nature of the transaction, and unlike government markets where the auction is the primary issue method, Eurobonds are typically issued under a *fixed price re-offer* method or a 'bought deal'. There is also a regulatory distinction as no one central authority is responsible for regulating the market and overseeing its structure. The true definition of a Eurobond is an international security that clears in one or both of the Euroclear and Clearstream settlement systems. It may be issued in the currency of the issuer's domicile.

Basic structure

A Eurobond is a debt capital market instrument issued in a 'Eurocurrency' through a syndicate of issuing banks and securities houses, that is distributed internationally when issued, sold in more than one country of issue and subsequently traded by market participants in several international financial centres. The Eurobond market is divided into sectors depending on the currency in which the issue is denominated. For example US dollar Eurobonds are often referred to as *Eurodollar* bonds, and similar sterling issues are called *Eurosterling* bonds. The prefix 'Euro' was first used to refer to deposits of US dollars in continental Europe in the 1960s. The Euro-deposit now refers to any deposit of a currency outside the country of issue of that currency, and is not limited to Europe.

For historical reasons and also because of the importance of the US economy and investor base, the major currency in which Eurobonds are denominated has always been US dollars. The dollar is followed by issues in euros, Japanese yen, sterling and a range of other currencies such as Australian, New Zealand and Canadian dollars, South African rand and so on. Issuers will denominate bonds in a currency that is attractive to particular investors at the time, and it is now more common for bonds to be issued in more 'exotic' currencies, such as East European, Latin American and Asian currencies.

The most common type of instrument issued in the Euro markets is the conventional vanilla bond, with fixed coupon and maturity date. Coupon frequency is annual. The typical face value of such Eurobonds is US$1000, €1000, £1000 or so on. The bond is unsecured, and therefore depends on the credit quality of its issuer in order to attract investors. Eurobonds have a typical maturity of five to ten years, although many high quality corporates have issued bonds with maturities of 30 years or even longer.

Eurobonds are not regulated by the country in whose currency the bonds are issued. They are typically registered on a national stock exchange, usually London or Luxemburg. Listing of the bonds enables certain institutional investors, who are prohibited from holding assets that are not listed on an exchange, to purchase them. The volume of trading on a registered stock exchange is negligible however; virtually all trading is on an OTC basis directly between market participants.

Interest on Eurobonds is paid gross and are free of any withholding or other taxes. This is one of the main features of Eurobonds, as is the fact that they are 'bearer' bonds, that is, there is no central register. Historically this meant that the bond certificates were bearer certificates with coupons attached; these days bonds are still designated 'bearer' instruments but are held in a central depository to facilitate electronic settlement.

Floating rate notes

An early innovation in the Eurobond market was the *floating rate note* (FRN). They are usually short to medium-dated issues, with interest quoted as a spread to a reference rate. The reference rate is usually the London interbank offered rate (LIBOR), or the Singapore interbank offered rate for issues in Asia (SIBOR). The euro interbank rate (EURIBOR) is also now commonly quoted. The spread over the reference rate is a function of the credit quality of the issuer, and can range from 10 to 150 basis points. Bonds typically pay a semi-annual coupon, although quarterly coupon bonds are also issued. The first FRN issue was by ENEL, an Italian utility company, in 1970. The majority of issuers are financial institutions such as banks and securities houses.

There are also perpetual, or undated, FRNs, the first issue of which was by National Westminster Bank plc in 1984. They are essentially similar to regular FRNs except that they have no maturity date and are therefore 'perpetual'. Most perpetual FRNs are issued by banks, for which they are attractive because they are a means of raising capital similar to equity but with the tax advantages associated with debt. They also match the payment characteristics of the banks assets. Traditionally the yield on perpetuals is higher than on both conventional bonds and fixed-term FRNs.

Zero-coupon bonds

An innovation in the market from the late 1980s was the *zero-coupon bond*, or *pure discount* bond, which makes no interest payments. Like zero-coupon bonds initially in government markets, the main attraction of these bonds for investors was that, as no interest was payable, the return could be declared entirely as capital gain, thus allowing the bondholder to avoid income tax. Most jurisdictions including the USA and UK have adjusted their tax legislation so that the return on zero-coupon bonds now counts as income and not capital gain.

CREDIT RATINGS

The risks associated with holding a fixed interest debt instrument are closely connected to the ability of the issuer to maintain the regular coupon payments as well as redeem the debt on maturity. Essentially the *credit risk* is the main risk of holding a bond. Only the highest-quality government debt, and a small number of supra-national and corporate debt, may be considered to be entirely free of credit risk. Therefore at any time the yield on a bond reflects investors' views on the ability of the issuer to meet its liabilities as set out in the bond's terms and conditions. A delay in paying a cash liability as it becomes due is known as technical default, and is a cause for extreme concern for investors; failure to pay will result in the matter being placed in the hands of the legal court as investors seek to recover their funds.

To judge the ability of an issue to meet its obligations for a particular debt issue, for the entire life of the issue, requires judgemental analysis of the issuer's financial strength and business prospects. There are a number of factors that must be considered, and larger banks, fund managers and corporates carry out their own *credit analysis* of individual borrowers' bond issues. The market also makes considerable use of the formal *credit ratings* that are assigned to individual bond issues by credit rating agencies. In the international markets arguably the two most influential rating agencies are Standard & Poors Corporation (S&P) and Moody's Investors Service, Inc (Moody's), based in the USA. FitchIBCA is also influential.

The specific factors that are considered by a rating agency, and the methodology used in conducting the analysis, differ slightly among the individual rating agencies. Although in many cases the ratings assigned to a particular issue by different agencies are the same, they occasionally differ, and in these instances investors usually seek to determine what aspect of an issuer is given more weight in an analysis by which individual agency.

Note that a credit rating is not a recommendation to buy (or equally, sell) a particular bond, nor is it a comment on market expectations. Credit analysis does take into account general market and economic conditions, but the overall point of credit analysis is to consider the financial health of the issuer and its ability to meet the obligations of the specific issue being rated. Credit ratings play a large part in the decision making of investors, and also have a significant impact on the interest rates payable by borrowers.

Some basics

A credit rating is a formal opinion given by a rating agency, of the *credit risk* for investors in a particular issue of debt securities. Ratings are given to public issues of debt securities by any type of entity, including governments, banks and corporates. They are also given to short-term debt such as commercial paper as well as bonds and medium-term notes.

Purpose of credit ratings

Investors in securities accept the risk that the issuer will default on coupon payments or fail to repay the principal in full on the maturity date. Generally credit risk is greater for securities with a long maturity, as there is a longer period for the issuer potentially to default. For example if company issues ten-year bonds, investors cannot be certain that the company will still exist in ten years' time. It may have failed and gone into liquidation some time before that. That said, there is also risk attached to short-dated debt securities, indeed there have been instances of default by issuers of commercial paper, which is a very short-term instrument.

The prospectus or offer document for an issue provides investors with some information about the issuer so that some credit analysis can be performed on the issuer before the bonds are placed. The information in the offer documents enables investors themselves to perform their own credit analysis by studying this information before deciding whether or not to invest. Credit assessments take up time, however, and also require the specialist skills of credit analysts. Large institutional investors do in fact employ such specialists to carry out credit analysis. However often it is too costly and time-consuming to assess every issuer in every debt market. Therefore investors commonly employ two other methods when making a decision on the credit risk of debt securities: name recognition and formal credit ratings.

Name recognition is when the investor relies on the good name and reputation of the issuer, and accepts that the issuer is of such good financial standing, or sufficient financial standing, that a default on interest and principal payments is highly unlikely. The Barings experience showed that this approach was not without its risks, however. In the sterling market, the building societies have a sufficiently high-quality reputation, as well as a history that is completely devoid of default, to make name recognition an acceptable ratings method.

Formal credit ratings

The request to an agency for a rating comes from the organisation planning the issue of bonds. Although ratings are provided for the benefit of investors, the issuer must bear the cost. However it is in the issuer's interest to request a rating as it raises the profile of the bonds, and investors may refuse to buy paper that is not accompanied with a recognised rating. Although the rating exercise involves a credit analysis of the issuer, the rating is applied to a specific debt issue. This means that in theory the credit rating is applied not to an organisation itself, but to specific debt securities that the organisation has issued or is planning to issue. In practice it is common for the market to refer to the creditworthiness of organisations themselves in terms of the rating of their debt. A highly-rated company such as Commerzbank is therefore referred to as a 'triple-A rated' company, although it is actually the bank's debt issues that are rated as triple-A.

The rating for an issue is kept constantly under review, and if the credit quality of the issuer declines or improves, the rating will be changed accordingly. An agency may announce in advance that it is reviewing a particular credit rating, and may go further and state that the review is a precursor to a possible downgrade or upgrade. This announcement is referred to as putting the issue under *credit watch*. The outcome of a credit watch is in most cases likely to be a rating downgrade, although the review might reaffirm the current rating or possibly upgrade it. During the credit watch phase the agency will advise investors to use the current rating with caution.

When an agency announces that an issue is under credit watch, the price of the bonds will fall in the market as investors look to sell their holdings. This upward movement in yield will be more pronounced if an actual downgrade results. For example in October 1992 the government of Canada was placed under credit watch and subsequently lost its AAA credit rating; as a result there was an immediate and sharp sell-off in Canadian government Eurobonds, before the rating agencies announced the actual results of their credit review.

Credit ratings vary between agencies. Separate categories are used by each agency for short-term debt (with original maturity of 12 months or less) and long-term debt of over one year original maturity. It is also usual to distinguish between higher 'investment grade' ratings where the credit risk is low and lower quality 'speculative grade' ratings, where the credit risk is greater. High-yield bonds are speculative-grade bonds and are generally rated no higher than double-B, although some issuers have been upgraded to tripe-B in recent years and a triple-B rating is still occasionally awarded to a high-yield bond.

A summary of long-term ratings is shown in Table 5.2. What do the ratings mean? Beyond the formal definitions given alongside the rating category, we can consider the statistical probability of default for bonds of each rating. This is shown in Table 5.3 for bonds during the period 1920–99, as published by Moody's. In other words, Ba-rated bonds had a 10.04 per cent chance of going into default over a five-year period. This may seem low, and worth the extra coupon that a Ba-rated bond would pay, but it's a one-shot deal: if it does default, you've lost your shirt.

However Table 5.2 does show us that the risk with some corporate bonds is worth it. For instance, the UK clearing banks are rated in the AA category, and we are happy to deposit our savings with them. So we should be happy holding their bonds, and you might well judge the small additional risk to be well worth the extra yield you can obtain from them, compared with the yield on gilts.

Notes

1 The term *technical default* is used to refer to non-payment or delay of a coupon as it becomes due, when the issuer is still otherwise financially solvent.
2 If the bank cannot sell an entire issue to its customers or other institutions in the market, it will take the remaining stock onto its own books. The fee payable by the borrower is compensation to the bank for taking on this underwriting risk.
3 There is a great moment in the film *Mission Impossible* (1996) when Tom Cruise says to Vanessa Redgrave that he requires payment in the form of Treasury securities 'with coupons attached'. This is wonderfully out of date!
4 The first offer of zero-coupon bonds was by J.C. Penney Co, Inc in the domestic US market in 1981.
5 It is my favourite at any rate. I've done very well out of Skipton BS PIBS, which I still hold, purchased at £123 and once trading as high as £214.
6 In 1980 there were nearly 200 building societies in the UK. At October 1999 this number had been reduced to 69, with another society (Bradford & Bingley) in the process of converting to a publicly listed bank. Many of the largest institutions, such as the Halifax, Woolwich and Alliance & Leicester building societies, had earlier converted to banks. The oldest surviving building society, the Chesham Building Society, dates from 1845.

Fitch	Moody's	Standard & Poors	Summary description
Investment grade: high credit quality			
AAA	Aaa	AAA	Gilt edged, prime, lowest risk, risk-free
AA+	Aa1	AA+	
AA	Aa2	AA	High-grade, high credit quality
AA-	Aa3	AA-	
A+	A1	A+	
A	A2	A	Upper-medium grade
A-	A3	A-	
BBB+	Baa1	BBB+	
BBB	Baa2	BBB	Lower-medium grade
BBB-	Baa3	BBB-	
Speculative: lower credit quality			
BB+	Ba1	BB+	
BB	Ba2	BB	Low grade; speculative
BB-	Ba3	BB-	
B+	B1	B+	
B	B2	B	Highly speculative
B-	B3	B-	
Highly speculative, substantial risk or in default			
		CCC+	
CCC	Caa	CCC	Considerable risk, in poor standing
		CCC-	
CC	Ca	CC	May already be in default, very speculative
C	C	C	Extremely speculative
		CI	Income bonds: no interest being paid
DDD			
DD			Default
D		D	

TABLE 5.2 Summary of credit rating agency bond ratings

Source: Rating agencies.

Bonds

| TABLE 5.3 Probability of default of corporate bonds across ratings categories |||||||
Rating period (years)	Aaa	Aa	A	Baa	Ba	B
1	0	0.08	0.08	0.3	1.43	4.48
2	0	0.25	0.27	0.94	3.45	9.16
3	0.02	0.41	0.6	1.73	5.57	13.73
4	0.09	0.61	0.97	2.62	7.8	17.56
5	0.2	0.97	1.37	3.51	10.04	20.89
6	0.31	1.37	1.78	4.45	12.09	23.68
7	0.43	1.81	2.23	5.34	13.9	26.19
8	0.62	2.26	2.63	6.21	15.73	28.32
9	0.83	2.67	3.1	7.12	17.31	30.22
10	1.09	3.1	3.61	7.92	19.05	31.9
15	1.89	5.61	6.13	11.46	25.95	39.17
20	2.38	6.75	7.47	13.95	30.82	43.7

Source: Moody's. Reproduced with permission.

CHAPTER 6

Understanding and appreciating the yield curve

Anyone with an involvement in the bond markets must become keenly interested in the yield curve. This applies whether one is a bond trader or bond investor, or even if one is just a student of the markets. The yield curve is the most important indicator in the bond market. As a private investor, it will help greatly your understanding and appreciation of bonds if you understand, and follow, the yield curve.[1] In this chapter I shall describe and explain the yield curve, and then look at its importance for the private investor. (This is rather more technical than other chapters in the book, and sources named are listed in the references at the end of the chapter, on page 136.)

INTRODUCTION

We have already considered the main measure of return associated with an investment in bonds, which is the *yield to maturity* or *gross redemption yield*. In most bond markets there are usually a large number of bonds trading at one time, at different yields and with varying terms to maturity. Investors and traders frequently examine the relationship between the yields on bonds that are in the same class. (By this we mean bonds that all have the same credit risk.) Plotting the yield of bonds that differ only in their term to maturity produces a graph that is known as a *yield curve*. The yield curve is an important indicator and knowledge source of the state of a debt capital market. It is sometimes referred to as the *term structure of interest rates* but strictly speaking this is not correct, as this term should be reserved for the zero-coupon yield curve only. We don't need to worry about this.

The analysis and pricing activity that takes place in the bond markets revolves around the yield curve. The yield curve describes the relationship between a particular redemption yield and a bond's maturity. Plotting the yields of bonds along the maturity structure will give us our yield curve. It is very important that only bonds from the same class of issuer or with the same degree of liquidity are used when plotting the yield curve: for example a curve might be constructed for UK gilts or for AA-rated sterling Eurobonds, but not a mixture of both, because gilts and Eurobonds are bonds from different class issuers.

The primary yield curve in any domestic capital market is the government bond yield curve, so for example in the US market it is the US Treasury yield curve. With the advent of the euro in the EU, in theory any euro-currency government bond can be used to plot a euro yield curve. In practice only bonds from the same government are used, as for various reasons different country bonds within euroland trade at slightly different yields. Outside the government bond markets, yield curves are plotted for Eurobonds, money market instruments, off-balance sheet instruments, in fact virtually all debt market instruments. So it is always important to remember to compare like for like when analysing yield curves across markets.

WHAT IS THE YIELD CURVE?

The yield curve is a graph that plots the yield of various bonds against their term to maturity. In other words, it is a snapshot of the current level of yields in the market. It is not an historical graph: that is, it does not show the level of yields over time. That would be a historical price (or yield) chart.

Yield curves are like football: very easy to grasp the basics, but devilishly complicated to become expert at (think Sunday-morning park football team against a team that included David Beckham, Steven Gerrard and Michael Owen). Just imagine you looked up gilt yields in the *Financial Times* on a day in August 2004 and saw this:

Gilt	Red yield[2]
Tr 8pc 03	3.79
Tr 5pc 04	4.00
Tr 7¼pc 07	4.62
Tr 5pc 12	4.70
Tr 8¾pc 17	4.74
Tr 8pc 21	4.68
Tr 4¼pc 32	4.52

This table shows the yields for gilts of 1, 2, 5, 10, 15, 20 and 30-year maturity (the 8% 2021 gilt is slightly under 20 years maturity but will do for our purposes – there is no gilt that matures in 2024 at the time we are looking at this).

We open up Microsoft Excel®[3] and write down two columns, one for 'maturity' and one for 'yield'. The years to maturity column forms the x-axis of the graph while the yield forms the y-axis. Then we use the Excel 'chart wizard' and it plots our graph for us! The result is as shown in Figure 6.1.

This curve looks about right. Intuitively, we would expect that yields would increase, the greater the maturity. Think about it: if you lent one person some money for one year and another person the same amount of money for ten years, would you charge them the same interest (assuming both presented the same credit risk)? No, you would as likely charge a higher rate to the ten-year chap, for two reasons. First, inflation will erode the value of your loan over the longer term, and second, while the longer-dated borrower might have the same credit quality as the short-dated borrower, there are other risks: for instance he might not be around in ten years' time. For these reasons, as a lender you need a higher return the further out you lend money.

So this gives us the *positively sloping* yield curve we see in Figure 6.1. But then, if that is the case, why does the curve not continue to slop upwards, all the way to the 30-year mark? The rate of upward movement drops after the five-year mark, and then actually falls to the 30-year point. This is a peculiarity of many markets: the 30-year bond, commonly called the *long bond*, is usually in such great demand among institutional investors such as pension funds that demand outstrips

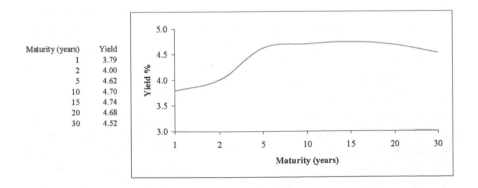

Figure 6.1 Creating a yield curve in Excel®

supply. As a result, the price of this bond is forced upwards, and as you should remember from Chapter 2, this moves the yield down to below what it should be.

It is fun to plot yield curves like this, and also interesting to see how they change in shape from day to day and over the longer term. Obviously if you are reliant on newspapers to obtain the relevant yields, you will always be using historical information, even if it's just one day old. But that should not worry you as a private investor.

Constructing a yield curve in the wholesale markets is a little more involved than we have described above, and a very complicated branch of mathematics is employed to derive the models used to fit yield curves. Is this relevant to the private investor? No. So let's move on.[4]

USING THE YIELD CURVE

The yield curve tells us where the bond market is trading now. It also implies the level of trading for the future, or at least what the market thinks will be happening in the future. In other words, it is a good indicator of the future level of the market. It is also a much more reliable indicator than any other used by private investors, and we can prove this empirically. But for the moment, take my word for it!

As an introduction into yield curve analysis, let us first consider its main uses. All participants in the debt capital markets will be interested in the current shape and level of the yield curve, as well as what this information implies for the future. The main uses are summarised below.

Setting the yield for all debt market instruments

The yield curve essentially fixes the price of money over the maturity structure. The yields of government bonds, from the shortest-maturity instrument to the longest, set the benchmark for yields for all other debt instruments in the market, around which all debt instruments are priced. What does this mean? Essentially it means that if a government five-year bond is trading at a yield of 5.00 per cent, all other five-year bonds, whoever they are issued by, will be issued to a yield over 5.00 per cent. The amount over 5.00 per cent at which the other bond trades is known as the *spread*. Therefore issuers of debt use the yield curve to price bonds and all other debt instruments. Generally the zero-coupon yield curve is used to price new issue securities, rather than the redemption yield curve (see later).

Acting as an indicator of future yield levels

As I discuss later in this chapter, the yield curve assumes certain shapes in response to market expectations of future interest rates. Bond market participants analyse the present shape of the yield curve in an effort to determine the implications regarding the direction of market interest rates. This is perhaps one of the most important functions of the yield curve. Interpreting it is a mixture of art and science. The yield curve is scrutinised for its information content not just by bond traders and fund managers but also by corporate financiers as part of their project appraisal. Central banks and government treasury departments also analyse the yield curve for its information content, regarding not just forward interest rates but also inflation levels. They then use this information when setting interest rates for the whole country. (Or, in the case of the European Central Bank, for a whole continent. This illustrates the importance and relevance of the yield curve to us all.)

Measuring and comparing returns across the maturity spectrum

Portfolio managers use the yield curve to assess the relative value of investments across the maturity spectrum. The yield curve indicates the returns that are available at different maturity points, and is therefore very important to fixed-interest fund managers, who can use it to assist them to assess which point of the curve offers the best return relative to other points.

Indicating relative value between different bonds of similar maturity

The yield curve can be analysed to indicate which bonds are 'cheap' or 'dear' (expensive) relative to the curve. Remember the 30-year bond yield we plotted in Figure 6.1? Its position on the curve indicated it was trading dear to the curve (because the yield was below where it 'should' be). Placing bonds relative to the *zero-coupon yield curve* helps to highlight which bonds should be bought or sold either outright or as part of a bond spread trade. What is the zero-coupon curve? I'll tell you in a moment.

Pricing interest-rate derivative instruments

The price of derivatives such as futures and swaps revolves around the yield curve. At the short end, products such as forward rate agreements are priced off the futures curve, but futures rates reflect the market's view on forward three-month cash deposit rates. At the longer end, interest-rate swaps are priced off the yield curve, while hybrid instruments that incorporate an option feature such as convertibles and callable bonds also reflect current yield curve levels. The 'risk-free' interest rate, which is one of the parameters used in option pricing, is the T-bill rate or short-term government repo rate, both constituents of the money market yield curve.

YIELD TO MATURITY YIELD CURVE

Yield curve shapes

The most commonly occurring yield curve is the yield to maturity yield curve. An explanation of how we calculate the yield to maturity was given in Chapter 2. The curve itself is constructed by plotting the yield to maturity against the term to maturity for a group of bonds of the same class.

We introduced a positively sloping yield curve earlier. Curves assume many different shapes, and in Figure 6.2 we show three hypothetical types. Bonds used in constructing the curve will only rarely have an exact number of whole years to redemption; however it is common to see yields plotted against whole years on the x-axis. This is because once a bond is designated the benchmark for that term, its yield is taken to be the representative yield. For example, the ten-year benchmark bond in 2005 in the UK gilt market, the 4.75% Treasury 2015, will maintain its benchmark status throughout 2006, even as its term to maturity falls below ten years. It loses benchmark status once a new benchmark for that maturity is issued.

The yield to maturity yield curve is the most commonly observed curve simply because yield to maturity is the most frequent measure of return used. The business sections of daily newspapers, where they quote bond yield at all, usually quote bond yields to maturity.

Now the caveat

This is one of those subjects that we need to be aware of and then promptly forget, a bit like in the world of cricket, when in the beginning your games master at school told you 'you must always walk if you know you are out' but in the real world you stand your ground until given out by the umpire!

The yield to maturity yield curve contains some inaccuracies. This is because the yield to maturity measure has one large weakness, which is the assumption of a constant discount rate for coupons during the bond's life at

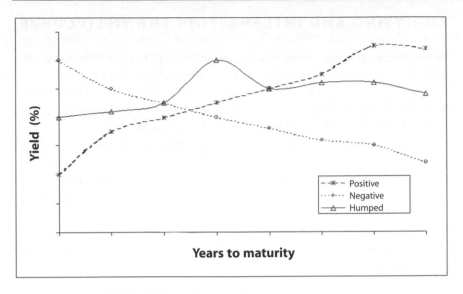

Figure 6.2 Yield to maturity yield curves

the redemption yield level. In other words, we discount all the cash flows of the bond at one discount rate. This is not a realistic assumption to make because we know, just as the night follows day, that interest rates in six months' time, used to discount the coupon due in six months, will not be the same as interest rate prevailing in two years' time (used to discount the two-year coupon). But we make this assumption nevertheless for the sake of convenience. The upshot of all this is that the redemption yield is not a true interest rate for its particular maturity.

By the way, this gives rise to a feature known as *reinvestment risk*, which is the risk that when we reinvest each bond coupon as it is paid, the interest rate at which we invest it will not be the same as the redemption yield prevailing on the day we bought the bond. We must accept this risk, unless we buy a *strip* or *zero-coupon bond*. Only zero-coupon bondholders avoid reinvestment risk as no coupon is paid during the life of their bond.

For the reasons we have discussed, the professional wholesale market often uses other types of yield curve for analysis when the yield to maturity yield curve is deemed unsuitable, usually the zero-coupon yield curve. This is the yield curve constricted from zero-coupon yields and is also known as the term structure of interest rates. We can construct a zero-coupon curve from bond prices and redemption yields, but as private investors we don't need to worry about this. If you are interested, there is a chat about it in Appendix 6.1.

ANALYSING AND INTERPRETING THE YIELD CURVE

From observing yield curves in different markets at any time, we notice that a yield curve can adopt one of four basic shapes, which are:

■ *normal* or *conventional*: in which yields are at 'average' levels and the curve slopes gently upwards as maturity increases
■ *upward sloping* or *positive* or *rising*: in which yields are at historically low levels, with long rates substantially greater t*han short rates*
■ *downward sloping or inverted* or *negative*: in which yield levels are very high by historical standards, but long-term yields are significantly lower than short rates
■ *humped*: where yields are high with the curve rising to a peak in the medium-term maturity area, and then sloping downwards at longer maturities.

Sometimes yield curves will incorporate a mixture of the above features. A great deal of effort is spent by bond analysts and economists analysing and interpreting yield curves. There is considerable information content associated with any curve at any time. For example Figure 6.3 shows the UK gilt redemption yield curve at three different times in the ten years from June

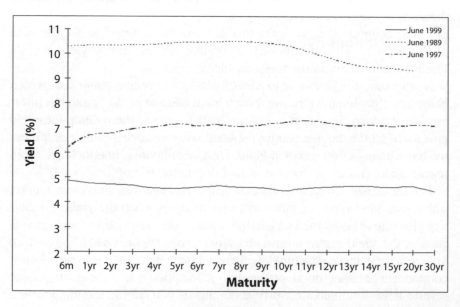

Figure 6.3 UK gilt redemption yield curves

1989 to June 1999. The shape of each curve tell its own story about the UK debt market and the UK economy at that particular time.

The existence of a yield curve itself indicates that there is a cost associated with funds of different maturities, otherwise we would observe a flat yield curve. The fact that we very rarely observe anything approaching a flat yield suggests that investors require different rates of return depending on the maturity of the instrument they are holding. In the next section we shall consider the various explanations that have been put forward to explain the shape of the yield curve at any one time. Why do we need to do this? Because an understanding of why the yield curve assumes certain shapes will help us to understand the information that a certain shape implies.

None of the theories can adequately explain everything about yield curves and the shapes they assume at any time, so generally observers seek to explain specific curves using a combination of the accepted theories.

THEORIES OF THE YIELD CURVE

To be honest, you don't really need to know this bit. You can go straight to the section on 'using the yield curve as a private investor' (page 129). But it's actually quite interesting and will help your understanding, so that's why I've included it here.

The expectations hypothesis

The expectations hypothesis suggests that bondholders' expectations determine the course of future interest rates. There are two main competing versions of this hypothesis, the *local expectations hypothesis* and the *unbiased expectations hypothesis*. The *return to maturity expectations hypothesis* and *yield to maturity expectations hypothesis* are also cited. (See Jonathan Ingersoll's *Theory of Financial Decision Making* (1987) for more about this.)

The local expectations hypothesis states that all bonds of the same class but differing in term to maturity will have the same expected holding period rate of return. This suggests that a six-month bond and a 20-year bond will produce the same rate of return, on average, over the stated holding period. So if you intend to hold a bond for six months, you will get the same return no matter what specific bond you buy. I feel this is not always the case, despite being mathematically neat. However it is worth spending a few moments discussing it and related points. Generally *holding period returns* from longer-dated bonds are on average higher than those from short-dated bonds. Intuitively we would expect this, with longer-dated bonds offering higher returns to compensate for their higher price volatility (risk). The local expectations hypothesis would not agree with the conventional belief that investors, being risk averse, require higher returns as a reward for taking on higher risk. In addition it does not provide any insight about the shape of the yield curve. Essentially though, in theory we should expect that the return from holding any bond for a six-month period will be the same irrespective of the term to maturity and yield that that bond has at time of purchase.

In his excellent book *Modelling Fixed Income Securities* (1996, p. 50), Professor Robert Jarrow states

> in an economic equilibrium, the returns on ... similar maturity zero-coupon binds cannot be too different. If they were too different, no investor would hold the bond with the smaller return. This difference could not persist in an economic equilibrium.

This is true, but in practice other factors can impact on holding period returns between bonds that do not have similar maturities. For instance investors will have restrictions as to which bonds they can hold, for example banks and building societies are required to hold short-dated bonds for liquidity purposes. In an environment of economic disequilibrium, these investors would still have to hold shorter-dated bonds, even if the holding period return was lower.

This is noted by Mark Rubinstein, who states in his book *Rubinstein on Derivatives* (1999, pp. 84–5):

> In the real world ... it is usually the case that annualised shorter-term riskless returns are lower than longer-term riskless returns .... Real assets with shorter-term payouts will tend to have a 'liquidity' advantage. In aggregate this advantage will be passed on to shorter-term financial claims on real assets [which results in them having a lower return].

A related theory is the *pure* or *unbiased expectations hypothesis*, which states that current implied forward rates are unbiased estimators of future spot interest rates.[5] It assumes that investors act in a way that eliminates any advantage of holding instruments of a particular maturity. Therefore if we have a positive-sloping yield curve, the unbiased expectations hypothesis states that the market expects spot interest rates to rise. Equally, an inverted yield curve is an indication that spot rates are expected to fall. If short-term interest rates are expected to rise, then longer yields should be higher than shorter ones to reflect this. If this were not the case, investors would only buy the shorter-dated bonds and roll over the investments when they matured. Likewise if rates are expected to fall, longer yields should be lower than short yields. The unbiased expectations hypothesis states that the long-term interest rate is a geometric average of expected future short-term rates.

Using elementary mathematics we can prove this theory. Indeed its premise must be so, to ensure no *arbitrage* opportunities exist in the market. The hypothesis can be used to explain any shape in the yield curve. Therefore a rising yield curve is explained by investors expecting short-term interest rates to rise. A falling yield curve is explained by investors expecting short-term rates to be lower in the future. A humped yield curve is explained by investors expecting short-term interest rates to rise and long-term rates to fall. *Expectations*, or views on the future direction of the market, are a function mainly of the expected rate of inflation. If the market expects inflationary pressures in the future, the yield curve will be positively shaped, while if inflation expectations are inclined towards disinflation, then the yield curve will be negative. Several empirical studies including one by Fama (1976) have shown that forward rates are essentially biased predictors of future spot interest rates, and often over-estimate future levels of spot rates.

The unbiased expectations hypothesis has also been criticised for suggesting that investors can forecast (or have a view on) very long-dated spot interest rates, which might be considered slightly unrealistic. As yield curves in most developed country markets exist to a maturity of up to 30 years or longer, such criticisms may have some substance. Are investors able to forecast interest rates 10, 20 or 30 years into the future? Perhaps not. Nevertheless this is indeed the information content of say, a 30-year bond. Since the yield on the bond is set by the market, it is valid to suggest that the market has a view on inflation and future interest rates for up to 30 years forward.

The expectations hypothesis is stated in more than one way; we have already encountered the local expectations hypothesis. Other versions include the *return to maturity* expectations hypothesis, which states that the total return from a holding a zero-coupon bond to maturity will be equal to the total return that is generated by holding a short-term instrument and continuously rolling it over the same maturity period. A related version, the *yield to maturity* hypothesis, states that the periodic return from holding a zero-coupon bond will be equal to the return from rolling over a series of coupon bonds, but refers to the annualised return earned each year rather than the total return earned over the life of the bond. This assumption enables a zero-coupon yield curve to be derived from the redemption yields of coupon bonds. The unbiased expectations hypothesis of course states that forward rates are equal to the spot rates expected by the market in the future. An article by Cox, Ingersoll and Ross (1981) suggests that only the local expectations hypothesis describes a model that is purely arbitrage-free, as under the other scenarios it would be possible to employ certain investment strategies that would produce returns in excess of what was implied by today's yields. Although it has been suggested that the differences between the local and the unbiased hypotheses are not material, a model that describes such a scenario would not reflect investors' beliefs, which is why further research is required in this area.[6]

The unbiased expectations hypothesis does not by itself explain all the shapes of the yield curve or the information content contained within it, which is why it is often combined with other explanations when seeking to explain the shape of the yield curve, including the liquidity preference theory.

Liquidity preference theory

Intuitively we might feel that longer-maturity investments are more risky than shorter ones. An investor lending money for a five-year term will usually demand a higher rate of interest than if she were to lend the same customer money for a five-week term. This is because the borrower might not be able to repay the loan over the longer time period as he might for instance, go bankrupt in that period. For this reason longer-dated yields should be higher than short-dated yields, to recompense the lender for the higher risk exposure during the term of the loan.[7]

We can consider this theory in terms of inflation expectations as well. Where inflation is expected to remain roughly stable over time, the market would anticipate a positive yield curve. However the expectations hypothesis cannot by itself explain this phenomenon, as under stable inflationary conditions one would expect a flat yield curve. The risk inherent in longer-dated investments, or the *liquidity preference theory*, seeks to explain a positive-shaped curve. Generally borrowers prefer to borrow over as long a term as possible, while lenders will wish to lend over as short a term as possible. Therefore, as we first stated, lenders have to be compensated for lending over the longer term; this compensation is considered a premium for a loss in *liquidity* for the lender. The premium is increased the further the investor lends across the term structure, so that the longest-dated investments will, all else being equal, have the highest yield. So the liquidity preference theory states that the yield curve should almost always be upward sloping, reflecting bondholders' preference for the liquidity and lower risk of shorter-dated bonds. An inverted yield curve could still be explained by the liquidity preference theory when it is combined with the unbiased expectations hypothesis. A *humped* yield curve might be viewed as a combination of an inverted yield curve together with a positive-sloping liquidity preference curve.

The difference between a yield curve explained by unbiased expectations and an actual observed yield curve is sometimes referred to as the *liquidity premium*. This refers to the fact that in some cases short-dated bonds are easier to transact in the market than long-term bonds. It is difficult to quantify the effect of the liquidity premium, which in any case is not static and fluctuates over time. The liquidity premium is so called because, in order to induce investors to hold longer-dated securities, the yields on such securities must be higher than those available on short-dated securities, which are more liquid and may be converted into cash more easily. The liquidity premium is the compensation required for holding less-liquid instruments. If longer-dated securities then provide higher yields, as is suggested by the existence of the liquidity premium, they should generate on average higher total returns over an investment period. This is not consistent with the local expectations hypothesis.

Segmentation hypothesis

The capital markets are made up of a wide variety of users, each with different requirements. Certain classes of investors will prefer to deal at the short end of the yield curve, while others will concentrate on the longer end of the market. The segmented markets theory suggests that activity is concentrated in certain specific areas of the market, and that there are no inter-relationships between these parts of the market. The relative amounts of funds invested in each of the maturity spectrum cause differentials in supply and demand, which result in humps in the yield curve. That is, the shape of the yield curve is determined by supply and demand for certain specific-maturity investments, each of which has no reference to any other part of the curve.

For example banks and building societies concentrate a large part of their activity at the short end of the curve, as part of daily cash management (known as *asset and liability management*) and for regulatory purposes (known as *liquidity* requirements). Fund managers such as pension funds and insurance companies however are active at the long end of the market.

Few institutional investors have any preference for medium-dated bonds. This behaviour on the part of investors will lead to high prices (low yields) at both the short and long ends of the yield curve, and lower prices (higher yields) in the middle of the term structure.

Since according to the segmented markets hypothesis a separate market exists for specific maturities along the term structure, interest rates for these maturities are set by supply and demand.[8] Where there is no demand for a particular maturity, the yield will lie above other segments. Market participants do not hold bonds in any area of the curve outside their area of interest, so that short-dated and long-dated bond yields exist independently of each other.

The segmented markets theory is usually illustrated by reference to banks and life companies. Banks and building societies hold their funds in short-dated instruments, usually no longer than five years in maturity. This is because of the nature of retail banking operations, with a large volume of instant access funds being deposited at banks, and also for regulatory purposes. Holding short-term, liquid bonds enables banks to meet and sudden or unexpected demand for funds from customers. The classic theory suggests that as banks invest their funds in short-dated bonds, the yields on these bonds is driven down. When they then liquidate part of their holding, perhaps to meet higher demand for loans, the yields are driven up and prices of the bonds fall. This affects the short end of the yield curve but not the long end.

The segmented markets theory can be used to explain any particular shape of the yield curve, although it fits best perhaps with positive-sloping curves. However it cannot be used to *interpret* the yield curve whatever shape it may be, and therefore offers no information content during analysis. By definition the theory suggests that for investors, bonds with different maturities are not perfect substitutes for each other. This is because different bonds have different holding period returns.[9] As a result of bonds being imperfect substitutes, markets are segmented according to maturity.

The segmentations hypothesis is a reasonable explanation of certain features of a conventional positive-sloping yield curve, but by itself is not sufficient. There is no doubt that banks and building societies have a requirement to hold securities at the short end of the yield curve, as much for regulatory purposes as for yield considerations. However other investors are probably more flexible and will place funds where value is deemed to exist. The higher demand for benchmark securities does drive down yields along certain segments of the curve.

A slightly modified version of the market segmentation hypothesis is known as the *preferred habitat theory*. This suggests that different market participants have an interest in specified areas of the yield curve, but can be induced to hold bonds from other parts of the maturity spectrum if there is sufficient incentive. Hence banks may at certain times hold longer-dated bonds once the price of these bonds falls to a certain level, making the return on the bonds worth the risk involved in holding them. Similar considerations may persuade long-term investors to hold short-dated debt. So higher yields will be required to make bondholders shift out of their usual area of interest. This theory essentially recognises the flexibility that investors have, outside regulatory or legal requirements (such as the terms of an institutional fund's objectives), to invest in wherever in the yield curve they identify value.

Humped yield curves

When plotting a yield curve of all the bonds in a certain class, it is common to observe humped yield curves. There are variety of reasons that these occur. In line with the unbiased expectations hypothesis, humped curves will be observed when interest rates are expected to rise over the next several periods and then decline. On other occasions humped curves can result from skewed expectations of future interest rates. This is when the market believes that fairly constant future interest rates are likely, but also believes that there is a small probability of lower rates in the medium term. The other common explanation for humped curves is the preferred habitat theory.

The flat yield curve

The conventional theories do not seek to explain a flat yield curve. Although it is rare to observe flat curves in a market, certainly for any length of time, at times they do emerge in response to peculiar economic circumstances. In the conventional thinking, a flat curve is not tenable because investors should in theory have no incentive to hold long-dated bonds over shorter-dated bonds when there is no yield premium, so that as they sell off long-dated paper the yield at the long end should rise, producing an upward-sloping curve. In previous circumstances of a flat curve, analysts have produced different explanations.

In November 1988 the US Treasury yield curve was flat relative to the recent past; researchers contended that this was the result of the market's view that long-dated yields would fall as bond prices rallied upwards.[10] One recommendation is to buy longer maturities when the yield curve is flat, in anticipation of lower long-term interest rates, which is the direct opposite to the view that a flat curve is a signal to sell long bonds. In the case of the US market in 1988, long bond yields did in fact fall by approximately 2 per cent in the following 12 months. This would seem to indicate that a view of future long-term rates should be behind the decision to buy or sell long bonds, rather than the shape of the yield curve itself. A flat curve may well be more heavily influenced by supply and demand factors than anything else, with the majority opinion eventually winning out and forcing a change in the curve to a more conventional shape.

Further views on the yield curve

In this discussion we have assumed an economist's world of the *perfect market* (also sometimes called the *frictionless* financial market). Such a perfect capital market is characterised by:

- perfect information
- no taxes
- bullet maturity bonds
- no transaction costs.

Of course in practice markets are not perfect. However assuming perfect markets makes the discussion of the term structure easier to handle. When we analyse yield curves for their information content, we have to remember that the markets that they represent are not perfect, and that frequently we observe anomalies that are not explainable by the conventional theories.

At any one time it is probably more realistic to suggest that a range of factors contributes to the yield curve being one particular shape. For instance short-term interest rates are greatly influenced by the availability of funds in the money market. The slope of the yield curve (usually defined as the ten-year yield minus the three-month interest rate) is also a measure of the degree of tightness of government monetary policy. A low, upward-sloping curve is often thought to be a sign that an environment of cheap money, as a result of a more loose monetary policy, is to be followed by a period of higher inflation and higher bond yields. Equally a high downward-sloping curve is taken to mean that a situation of tight credit, caused by a more strict monetary policy, will result in falling inflation and lower bond yields.

Inverted yield curves have often preceded recessions. For instance the *Economist* in an article from April 1998 remarked that in the USA every recession since 1955 bar one has been preceded by a negative yield curve. The analysis is the same: if investors expect a recession they also expect inflation to fall, so the yields on long-term bonds will fall relative to short-term bonds. So the conventional explanation for an inverted yield curve is that the markets and the investment community expect a slowdown of the economy, if not outright recession.[11] In this case one would expect the regulatory authorities to ease the money supply by reducing the base interest rate in the near future: hence an inverted curve. At the same time, a reduction of short-term interest rates will affect short-dated bonds and these are sold off by investors, further raising their yield.

While the conventional explanation for negative yield curves is an expectation of economic slowdown, on occasion other factors are involved. In the UK in the period July 1997–June 1999 the gilt yield curve was inverted. There was no general view that the economy was heading for recession, however. In fact the new Labour government (or should that be New Labour?) inherited an economy believed to be in good health. Instead the explanation behind the inverted shape of the gilt yield curve focused on two other factors: first, the handing of responsibility for setting interest rates to the Monetary Policy Committee (MPC) of the Bank of England, and second, the expectation that the UK would over the medium term abandon sterling and join the euro. The yield curve in this time suggested that the market expected the MPC to be successful and keep inflation at a level around 2.5 per cent over the long term (its target at that time was actually a 1 per cent range either side of 2.5 per cent), and also that sterling interest rates would need to come down over the medium term as part of *convergence* with the conditions in the eurocurrency area. These are both medium-term expectations however, and in the author's view not tenable at the short end of the yield curve. In fact the term structure moved to a positive-sloped shape up to the six-to-seven-year area, before inverting out to the long end of the curve, in June 1999. By the beginning of 2002 it had assumed a conventional positive-sloping shape. This is a more logical shape for the curve to assume.

There is therefore significant information content in the yield curve, and economists and bond analysts will consider the shape of the curve as part of their policy making and investment advice. The shape of parts of the curve, such as the short or long end, as well that of the entire curve, can serve as an useful predictor of future market conditions.

As part of an analysis it is also worthwhile considering the yield curves across several different markets and currencies. For instance the interest-rate swap curve, and its position relative to the government bond yield curve, is also regularly analysed for its information content. In developed country economies the interest-rate swap market is invariably as liquid as the government bond market, if not more liquid, and so it is common to see the swap curve analysed when making predictions about say, the future level of short-term interest rates.[12]

Government policy will influence the shape and level of the yield curve, including policy on public sector borrowing, debt management and open-market operations. The market's perception of the size of public sector debt will influence bond yields; for instance an increase in the level of debt can lead to an increase in bond yields across the maturity range. Open-market operations, which refers to the daily operation by the Bank of England to control the level of the money supply (to which end the Bank purchases short-term bills and also engages in repo dealing), can have a number of effects. In the short term they can tilt the yield curve both upwards and downwards; longer term, changes in the level of the base rate will affect yield levels. An anticipated rise in base rates can lead to a drop in prices for short-term bonds, whose yields will be expected to rise; this can lead to a temporarily inverted curve. Finally, debt management policy will influence the yield curve. (In the UK this is now the responsibility of the Debt Management Office.) Much government debt is rolled over as it matures, but the maturity of the replacement debt can have a significant influence on the yield curve in the form of humps in the market segment in which the debt is placed, if the debt is priced by the market at a relatively low price and hence high yield.

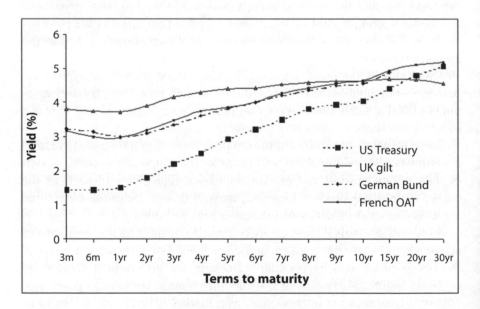

Figure 6.4 Government yield curves as at November 2002
Includes interpolated yields

Rate source: Bloomberg

USING THE YIELD CURVE AS A PRIVATE INVESTOR

I frequently get asked by people where I think the market is going, and whether now is a good time to buy or sell. The first thing I respond with is that one never knows: equities are such incomprehensible, not to mention unreliable, beasts.[13] I then point out that if they are looking for an indicator, or a crystal ball that will give them an idea of what the future holds, they are better off looking at the government bond yield curve. Here's why.

The yield curve, as we should have concluded from the foregoing, contains information that tells us what the market as a whole thinks of the market. Does this make sense? Yes, if you remember that *we are the market*. The universe of borrowers, lenders, banks, investors, traders, brokers, all the way from governments and global investment banks to the individual private saver: they all form the market. The general opinion of the market manifests itself in the shape of the yield curve.

So the yield curve is important to understand and follow because it is an indicator for use by investors. Its shape tells us things. For instance, we have seen that a gently positive-sloping curve is what we would expect. It reflects that lenders require higher return for longer-dated loans, because of the greater risk and expected inflation. It also indicates that short-term interest rates are expected to remain low, and not increase in the short term. An inverted curve would tend to indicate that short-term interest rates are high, or that they are expected to increase in the near term. The moment that a positive curve turns into an inverted one is a powerful signal from the market to the market.

There are a number of reasons why all investors should follow the yield curve. These include the following:

- Forecasting is quick and simple if you use the yield curve, and does not require sophisticated analysis.
- The simplicity of the yield curve, coupled with its reliability, means that it can be used to confirm conclusions you have obtained from other indicators. If what the curve is telling you does not tally with what you think other indicators are telling you, then you should question the conclusions you have drawn from the other indicators.
- The yield curve serves as a good indicator of market sentiment. As we noted above, its shape tells you what the market thinks.

The shape of the yield curve also reflects the following:

- Any anticipated changes made by the central bank to the base rate.

- The extent of the *risk premium* in holding longer-dated assets. If the curve is very positively sloped, the premium is high and investors are not too happy to hold long-dated bonds, if not, then not, and they are happy (which we would expect at times of a booming economy).
- When the curve is inverted, the extent of inversion presents clues on what the market expects the extent of any recession to be. The greater the inversion, the deeper the expected recession.

How much is much? That is, how do you know if a risk premium of 50 basis points is high? The only way to make sense of the extent of inversion or changes in yields is to compare them with historical values. Once you know what the curve looked like in the past, you'll be able to make sense of what it looks like now.

For these reasons you should make a point of following the curve on a regular basis. It is a reliable indicator, and a better predictor of the economy than the stock market or an equity index.[14] Let us view it as an old friend: God bless the yield curve!

APPENDIX 6.1: THE ZERO-COUPON YIELD CURVE

The *zero-coupon* (or spot) yield curve plots zero-coupon yields (or spot yields) against term to maturity. A zero-coupon yield is the yield prevailing on a bond that has no coupons. In the first instance if there is a liquid zero-coupon bond market we can plot the yields from these bonds if we wish to construct this curve. However it is not necessary to have a set of zero-coupon bonds in order to construct this curve, as we can derive it from a coupon or par yield curve. In fact in many markets where no zero-coupon bonds are traded, a spot yield curve is derived from the conventional yield to maturity yield curve. This is of course a *theoretical* zero-coupon (spot) yield curve, as opposed to the *market* or *observed* spot curve that can be constructed using the yields of actual zero-coupon bonds trading in the market.

Spot yields must comply with equation (6.1). This equation assumes annual coupon payments and that the calculation is carried out on a coupon date so that accrued interest is zero.

$$P_d = \sum_{n=1}^{N} \frac{C}{(1 + rs_n)^n} + \frac{M}{(1 + rs_T)^N}$$

$$= \sum_{n=1}^{N} C \times Df_n + M \times Df_N$$

(6.1)

where

rs_n is the spot or zero-coupon yield on a bond with t years to maturity
$Df_n \equiv 1/(1 + rs_n)^n$ = the corresponding *discount factor.*

In (6.1) rs_1 is the current one-year spot yield, rs_2 the current two-year spot yield, and so on. Theoretically the spot yield for a particular term to maturity is the same as the yield on a zero-coupon bond of the same maturity, which is why spot yields are also known as zero-coupon yields.

This last is an important result. It means spot yields can be derived from redemption yields that have been observed in the market.

As with the yield to redemption yield curve, the spot yield curve is commonly used in the market. It is viewed as the true term structure of interest rates because there is no reinvestment risk involved; the stated yield is equal to the actual annual return. That is, the yield on a zero-coupon bond of n years maturity is regarded as the true n-year interest rate. Because the observed government bond redemption yield curve is not considered to be the true interest rate, analysts often construct a theoretical spot yield curve. Essentially this is done by breaking down each coupon bond being observed into its constituent cash flows, which become a series of individual zero-coupon bonds. For example, £100 nominal of a 5% two-year bond (paying annual coupons) is considered equivalent to £5 nominal of a one-year zero-coupon bond and £105 nominal of a two-year zero-coupon bond.

Let us assume that in the market there are 30 bonds all paying annual coupons. The first bond has a maturity of one year, the second bond of two years, and so on out to 30 years. We know the price of each of these bonds, and we wish to determine what the prices imply about the market's estimate of future interest rates. We naturally expect interest rates to vary over time, but assume that all payments being made on the same date are valued using the same rate. For the one-year bond we know its current price and the amount of the payment (comprised of one coupon payment and the redemption proceeds) we shall receive at the end of the year; therefore we can calculate the interest rate for the first year. Let's assume the one-year bond has a coupon of 5 per cent. If the bond is priced at par and you invest £100 today you will receive £105 in one year's time, hence the rate of interest is apparent and is 5 per cent. For the two-year bond we use this interest rate to calculate the future value of its current price in one year's time: *this is how much you would receive if you had invested the same amount in the one-year bond.* However the two-year bond pays a coupon at the end of the first year; if we subtract this amount from the future value of the current price, the net amount is what you should be giving up in one year in return for the one remaining payment. From these numbers we can calculate the interest rate in year two.

Assume that the two-year bond pays a coupon of 6 per cent and is priced at £99.00. If the £99.00 was invested at the rate we calculated for the one-year bond (5 per cent), it would accumulate £103.95 in one year, made up of the £99 investment and interest of £4.95. On the payment date in one year's time, the one-year bond matures and the two-year bond pays a coupon of 6 per cent. If everyone expected that at this time the two-year bond would be priced at more than £97.95 (which is £103.95 minus £6.00), then no investor would buy the one-year bond, since it would be more advantageous to buy the two-year bond and sell it after one year for a greater return. Similarly if the price was less than £97.95 no investor would buy the two-year bond, as it would be cheaper to buy the shorter bond and then buy the longer-dated bond with the proceeds received when the one-year bond matures. Therefore the two-year bond must be priced at exactly £97.95 in 12 months' time. For this £97.95 to grow to £106.00 (the maturity proceeds from the two-year bond, comprising the redemption payment and coupon interest), the interest rate in year two must be 8.20 per cent We can check this using the present value formula covered earlier. At these two interest rates, the two bonds are said to be in equilibrium.

This is an important result, and shows that there can be no *arbitrage* opportunity along the yield curve; using interest rates available today the return from buying the two-year bond must equal the return from buying the one-year bond and rolling over the proceeds (or reinvesting) for another year. This is the known as the *breakeven principle*.

Using the price and coupon of the three-year bond we can calculate the interest rate in year three in precisely the same way. Using each of the bonds in turn, we can link together the *implied* one-year rates for each year up to the maturity of the longest-dated bond. The process is known as *boot-strapping*. The 'average' of the rates over a given period is the spot yield for that term: in the example given above, the rate in year one is 5 per cent, and in year two is 8.20 per cent. An investment of £100 at these rates would grow to £113.61. This gives a total percentage increase of 13.61 per cent over two years, or 6.588 per cent per annum (the average rate is not obtained by simply dividing 13.61 by 2, but – using our present value relationship again – by calculating the square root of '1 plus the interest rate' and then subtracting 1 from this number). Thus the one-year yield is 5 per cent and the two-year yield is 8.20 per cent.

In real-world markets it is not necessarily as straightforward as this; for instance on some dates there may be several bonds maturing, with different coupons, and on some dates there may be no bonds maturing. It is most unlikely that there will be a regular spacing of bond redemptions exactly one year apart. For this reason it is common for analysts to use a software model to calculate the set of implied spot rates which best fits the market prices of the bonds that do exist in the market. For instance if there are several one-year bonds, each of their prices may imply a slightly different rate of interest. We choose the rate which gives the smallest average price error. In practice all bonds are used to find the rate in year one, all bonds with a term longer than one year are used to calculate the rate in year two, and so on. The zero-coupon curve can also be calculated directly from the coupon yield curve using a method similar to that described above; in this case the bonds would be priced at par and their coupons set to the par yield values.

The zero-coupon yield curve is ideal to use when deriving implied forward rates, which we consider next, and defining the term structure of interest rates. It is also the best curve to use when determining the *relative value*, whether cheap or dear, of bonds trading in the market, and when pricing new issues, irrespective of their coupons. However it is not an absolutely accurate indicator of average market yields because most bonds are not zero-coupon bonds.

A hairy bit

Now I have introduced the concept of the zero-coupon curve, here is a more formal look at the mathematics involved. When deriving spot yields from redemption yields, we view conventional bonds as being made up of an *annuity*, which is the stream of fixed coupon payments, and a zero-coupon bond, which is the redemption payment on maturity. To derive the rates we can use (6.1), setting $P_d = M = 100$ and $C = rm_N$, as shown in (6.2) below. This has the coupon bonds trading at par, so that the coupon is equal to the yield.

$$100 = rm_N \times \sum_{n=1}^{N} Df_n + 100 \times D_N$$

$$= rm_N \times A_N + 100 \times D_N$$

(6.2)

where rm_N is the par yield for a term to maturity of N years, where the discount factor Df_N is the fair price of a zero-coupon bond with a par value of £1 and a term to maturity of N years, and where

$$A_N \times \sum_{n=1}^{N} Df_n = A_{N-1} + Df_N$$

(6.3)

is the fair price of an annuity of £1 per year for N years (with $A_0 = 0$ by convention). Substituting (6.3) into (6.2) and rearranging will give us the expression (6.4) for the N-year discount factor:

$$Df_N = \frac{1 - rm_N \times A_{N-1}}{1 + rm_N} \tag{6.4}$$

If we assume one-year, two-year and three-year redemption yields for bonds priced at par to be 5 per cent, 5.25 per cent and 5.75 per cent respectively, we obtain the following solutions for the discount factors.

$$Df_1 = \frac{1}{1 + 0.05} + 0.95238$$

$$Df_2 = \frac{1 - (0.0525)(0.95238)}{1 + 0.0525} + 0.90261$$

$$Df_3 = \frac{1 - (0.0575)(0.95238 + 0.90261)}{1 + 0.0575} + 0.84476$$

We can confirm that these are the correct discount factors by substituting them back into equation (6.2): this gives us the following results for the one-year, two-year and three-year par value bonds (with coupons of 5 per cent, 5.25 per cent and 5.75 per cent respectively):

$$100 = 105 \times 0.95238$$

$$100 = 5.25 \times 0.95238 + 105.25 \times 0.90261$$

$$100 = 5.75 \times 0.95238 + 5.75 \times 0.90261 + 105.75 \times 0.84476$$

Now that we have found the correct discount factors it is relatively straightforward to calculate the spot yields using equation (6.1), and this is shown below.

$$Df_1 = \frac{1}{(1 + rs_1)} = 0.95238 \text{ which gives } rs_1 = 5.0\%$$

$$Df_2 = \frac{1}{(1 + rs_2)^2} = 0.90261 \text{ which gives } rs_2 = 5.269\%$$

$$Df_3 = \frac{1}{(1 + rs_3)^3} = 0.84476 \text{ which gives } rs_3 = 5.778\%$$

Equation (6.1) discounts the n-year cash flow (comprising the coupon payment and/or principal repayment) by the corresponding n-year spot yield. In other words rs_n is the *time-weighted rate of return* on a n-year bond. Thus as we said in the previous section, the spot yield curve is the correct method for pricing or valuing any cash flow, including an irregular cash flow, because it uses the appropriate discount factors. That is, it matches each cash flow to the discount rate that applies to the time period in which the cash flow is paid. Compare this with the approach for the yield to maturity procedure discussed earlier, which discounts all cash flows by the same yield to maturity. This illustrates neatly why the n-period zero-coupon interest rate is the true interest rate for an N-year bond.

The expressions above are solved algebraically in the conventional manner, although those wishing to use a spreadsheet application such as Microsoft Excel® can input the constituents of each equation into individual cells and solve using the 'Tools' and 'Goal seek' functions.

Notes

1 I could talk for ever about the yield curve, it's a fascinating subject. I was teaching a course on bonds once and one of the delegates suggested (in jest, I hope!) that he would hate to attend a dinner party I hosted, as the walls of my house were probably decorated with pictures of yield curves. But notwithstanding the passion with which we should discuss the subject, the yield curve is far too important to be used as a source of art!
2 'Red' means redemption yield.
3 I have no hesitation in endorsing Microsoft Excel® as a superior product. I remember having to use Lotus1-2-3 in DOS when I first started work in the City!
4 But if you are interested, see my book *Advanced Fixed Income Analytics* (Butterworth Heinemann 2003), or better still *Analysing and Interpreting the Yield Curve* (Wiley Asia 2004).
5 For original discussion, see Lutz (1940) and Fisher (1986, although he formulated his ideas earlier).
6 For example Campbell (1986) and Livingstone (1990).
7 For original discussion, see Hicks (1946).
8 See Culbertson (1957).
9 Ibid.
10 See Levy (1999).
11 A recession is formally defined as two successive quarters of falling output in the domestic economy.
12 Interest rate swaps are derivative instruments used in the professional wholesale markets to change the basis of an interest rate liability, and also for speculative trading purposes. We don't need to worry about them.

13 Actually the second thing: these days one has to preface any such answer with the usual disclaimer about liability, and a reminder that my answer does not constitute 'investment advice'!

14 In his book *The Strategic Bond Investor* (2002), Anthony Crescenzi quotes a number of studies that prove the reliability of the yield curve in forecasting recessions and booms. For instance, the shape of the Treasury yield curve changed to predict the recessions in the USA in 1980, 1982 and 1989. Also, note the comment later about a similar observation in the *Economist*.

REFERENCES

Campbell, J., 'A defence of traditional hypotheses about the term structure of interest rates', *Journal of Finance*, March 1986, pp. 183–93.

Choudhry, M., 'The information content of the United Kingdom gilt yield curve', unpublished MBA assignment, Henley Management College, 1998.

Choudhry, M., *The Bond and Money Markets*, Butterworth Heinemann, 2001, chapters 51–53.

Cox, J., Ingersoll, J.E. and Ross, S.A., 'A re-examination of traditional hypothesis about the term structure of interest rates', *Journal of Finance* 36, September 1981, pp. 769–99.

Culbertson, J.M., 'The term structure of interest rates,' *Quarterly Journal of Economics* 71, November 1957, pp. 485–517.

Economist, 'Admiring those shapely curves,' 4 April 1998, p.117.

Fama, E.F., *'Forward rates as predictors of future spot interest rates'*, Journal of Financial Economics, Vol. 3, No. 4, October 1976, pp. 361–77.

Fama, E.F., 'The information in the term structure,' *Journal of Financial Economics* 13, December 1984, pp. 509–28.

Fisher, I., 'Appreciation of interest', *Publications of the American Economic Association*, August 1986, pp. 23–39.

Hicks, J., *Value and Capital*, Oxford University Press, 1946.

Ingersoll, J., *Theory of Financial Decision Making*, Rowman & Littlefield, 1987, chapter 18.

Jarrow, R., *Modelling Fixed Income Securities and Interest Rate Options*, McGraw-Hill, 1996.

Levy, H., *Introduction to Investments*, 2nd edn, South-Western, 1999.

Lutz, F., 'The structure of interest rates', *Quarterly Journal of Economics*, November 1940, pp. 36–63.

McCulloch, J.H., 'An estimate of the liquidity premium,' *Journal of Political Economy* 83, January–February 1975, pp. 95–119.

Meiselman, D., *The Term Structure of Interest Rates*, Prentice Hall, 1962.

Rubinstein, M., *Rubinstein on Derivatives*, RISK Publishing, 1999.

Sinclair, D., *The Pound*, Century, 2000.

(See also 'Further Reading' on page 163.)

CHAPTER 7

Dealing for the private investor

Private investors seem not to be intimidated about the prospect of dealing in shares. They may have an account with a stockbroker, perhaps over the telephone or Internet, or simply walk into a high-street bank and deal in person there. It should be no different with bonds. Some of the bonds I described in Chapters 4 and 5 may be a little difficult to get hold of, or to obtain prices for, but generally stockbrokers should be able to deal in them. In this chapter we talk about how one can deal in bonds. It's easy.

DEALING IN BONDS

Dealing language

When dealing in equities we mention numbers of shares. For instance, one might telephone a broker and, after checking the price, ask to buy 500 shares. If the shares are priced at £3.50, it is a simple calculation to check the cost. Add stamp duty, broker's commission, any extra charge if one still requests share certificates, and that's the total consideration.

Bonds are slightly different but no less straightforward. Let's imagine you have decided to invest in a gilt (surprise!), the 5% Treasury 2008.[1] Here's what you do after making your decision.

- You first establish contact with the broker, whether in person, over the telephone or the Internet. (If making a postal application, the procedure is essentially the same.) You quote the bond in terms of its issuer, coupon and maturity date. So in this case you would state 'UK gilt, 5% 2008'. Or you can say '5% Treasury 2008'.[2]
- You then state whether you wish to buy or sell.
- You then quote the nominal amount you wish to buy. This is where the language differs slightly from shares. Remember that bonds are quoted in terms of £100 per cent nominal. In some markets, for example the US domestic market, the convention is to quote in terms of US$1000 nominal. Say the price of the gilt you are buying is £98.75, and you wish to buy £5000 nominal; you must add the accrued interest when calculating

the consideration. The broker will usually confirm the number of days accrued and also tell you what it works out as. If the accrued is 0.55, you add this to the clean price to obtain a dirty price of £99.30. The bond consideration is then as we showed back in Chapter 2. Alternatively, you can tell the broker how much you wish to invest. So you could say, 'Buy 5% Treasury 2008, wish to invest £5000 total consideration.' This will include commission costs.

- Unlike shares, because of lower volatility levels it is not so vital to state a 'best' price at which you will be prepared to deal, if the broker cannot deal right away.
- You can also specify if you wish to switch out of one bond and into another, in which case the broker will calculate the amount of nominal of the stock being switched into after ascertaining the proceeds of the sold stock.

That's it, simple.

Dealing mechanics

The price you are quoted for a bond will be a two-way one, the bid price at which the stockbroker will pay for stock you are selling to him, and the offer price that you will pay if you wish to buy stock off the broker. Obviously the broker's bid price is lower than his offer price. It is possible to get an idea of how liquid a particular bond is from the 'spread' of its bid–offer quote. You will not know what constitutes a 'tight' (and therefore liquid) spread unless you compare it with other bond spreads. Generally gilt prices, and prices of bonds such as US Treasuries, are very liquid so they can serve as a benchmark for you.

There are a number of Internet stockbrokers that you can use to transact business in bonds. For instance Charles Schwab and CSFBDirect offer an online service that extends to government bonds, a large number of corporate bonds and Eurobonds. The service on both their sites is quite user-friendly, for example the customer can enter searches for bonds that meet specific criteria, look for recent issues and take part in forthcoming issue auctions. In continental Europe online brokers including eCortal and Comdirect offer a range of services for bonds.

STOCKBROKERS

Stockbrokers come in all kinds of shapes and sizes. They cater for a variety of customers. For instance, the branch of Killik and Co on Esher High

Street, Surrey, looks very upmarket and is furnished in the style of the drawing room of a country house. This presumably caters for the customer who wishes to have personal contact! There are a number of factors to consider when deciding how and with whom to deal. Let's consider them now.

Types of stockbroker

Essentially there are four types of stockbroker that you can consider:

Execution only

This refers to a broker who will simply take your order and place it in the market for you. He acts purely as an agent. The commission payable is the lowest available, and may be a flat fee per trade, or an order-value-based commission. Execution-only brokers include the 'no-frills' firms that have proliferated from the late 1990s and are exclusively telephone or Internet-based.

This service can be recommended for infrequent dealers or for experienced investors who are happy to make all their own decisions. They are perfectly suitable for dealing in bonds such as gilts, but more obscure bonds may present them with some difficulty.

Limited advice

This is one step higher than the execution-only service. The broker will come up with ideas, and run them past you when you get in touch. The final decision to deal remains with you. Commission is based on a percentage of deal value.

This service will provide some limited research (usually a one-page commentary; see Colin Smart's client newsletter page for Walker, Cripps, Weddle, Beck plc, which the author has been receiving since 1989. Not sure how that started!) and the broker will provide suggestions for dealing. Some brokers are more knowledgeable on bonds than others, so if you opt for this service make sure that it is with one who is! You'll soon be able to tell, once you start talking about the yield curve and the money supply.

Detailed advice

This is also known as portfolio advice-based broking. Here the broker provides advice on a portfolio basis, as part of a wider look at your overall investment strategy. The broker will be more familiar with your overall investment strategy and personal circumstances. Payment is typically a flat fee, usually annual, plus commission whenever dealing takes place.

The advice with this service will extend to tax affairs and such like. It is more expensive so only a higher-net-worth individual will be of interest to this type of broker.

Discretionary

This is provided by the traditional full-service stockbroker. You places your investment with the broker, who places it in the market, and in whichever instruments he sees fit. Of course the broker would have entered into a full 'know your customer' dialogue with you, so he or she will be aware of your needs and objectives. Commission is usually a percentage of the portfolio value.

This service is for high-net-worth individuals, and if your portfolio is below £50,000, there is little point in thinking of such a service.

Choosing a broker

A broker is, like many another personal service, such as hairdressing or retail banking, very much a matter of personal choice. It is a little more problematic for bond investors because so many brokers gear themselves to dealing in equities. If you are selecting a broker for the first time, it is probably worth approaching a few and assessing their response, their marketing, and so on. You may wish to look up some names via a trade association; for instance the Association of Private Client Investment Managers (APCIMS) contains information on its membership, largely stockbrokers, that will be of value. Its website is www.apcims.co.uk. You can then request information from the ones that appear to be most suitable from the APCIMS list.

Table 7.1 provides a list of UK-based stockbrokers that offer dealing services in sterling bonds. All the firms listed provide an Internet-based execution-only service.

PICKING SUITABLE BONDS

I wrote an earlier book called *The Bond and Money Market* (2001), which is not light reading – it has over 1100 pages. But it gives an indication of the depth and variety of the bond markets. They are incredibly diverse.

TABLE 7.1 Selected stockbrokers offering a dealing service in sterling bonds

Stock-broker	Discretionary service	Advisory service	European bonds	US bonds	Website
Barclays Stockbrokers	X	X	X	X	www.barclays-stockbrokers.co.uk
Cave & Sons	X	X	X	X	www.caves.co.uk
Charles Schwab Europe			X	X	www.schwab-global.com
Squaregain			X	X	www.squaregain.co.uk
James Brearley	X	X			www.jbrearley.co.uk
Killik & Co	X	X			www.killik.co.uk
NatWest Stockbrokers	X	X	X	X	www.natweststockbrokers.co.uk
Redmayne Bentley	X	X			www.redmayne.co.uk
Charles Stanley					www.fastrade.co.uk
Walker Crips Weddle Beck	X	X	X	X	www.wcwb.co.uk

There are a great many bonds that are not suitable for private investors (just as there are a great many equities that are not suitable for private investors). As I stated at the start of this book, some bonds, such as gilts or Treasuries, are plainly suitable for everybody. Beyond these instruments though, it becomes necessary to be sure about your objectives, as well as the bonds themselves, before going ahead and investing. The former is important because people at different stages of their lives will have different needs and requirements from their saving. My dictum from earlier in the book, that you should place a percentage of your savings in bonds that is equal to your age, is about right. This reflects the general belief that early in life you are saving for the long term, and for capital gain, while later in life interest income and preservation of capital is more important.

Let's look at how bonds fit into this general belief.

Income versus capital gain

The usual mantra is that equities equal capital gain and bonds equal income. This is too simplistic. You can make capital gains with bonds, as I have noted elsewhere in this book. But if you are looking for income, a high-coupon bond is suitable, although it will generally be priced above par and so (if held to maturity) produce a capital loss. If I were to target such a bond, it might be to an retired person on basic-rate tax who requires income from his or her savings.

Capital gains result when interest rates fall – pushing bond prices up – and so if you have bought at the top of the interest rate cycle this will prove beneficial. Remember that it is irrelevant whether you are looking to hold the bond to maturity. But if you have a view on interest rates, a short-term of holding of bonds can prove profitable provided you call the change in rates correctly.

Taxation issues

Here's where it starts to get complicated. Whether an investor is a basic or higher-rate taxpayer can be an important consideration. A higher-rate taxpayer would prefer a low-coupon bond, for instance. The *Financial Times* regularly presents details on bonds that are the best choice for low-rate and high-rate taxpayers. Taxpayers in the UK may also wish to 'wrap' a bondholding in a tax-free vehicle such as an Individual Savings Account (ISA), although amounts under an ISA scheme are limited.

I have only touched on the main issues involved. I hope that the general flavour has been positive, and that readers are now convinced about bonds.

In any event, it can be a great deal of fun finding about bonds and following their progress in the market. If only we could say that about equities!

At any rate let's go and have some fun.

Notes

1 The process described will be no different whichever bond you buy or sell, be it government or corporate bond.

2 Gilt market professionals would say 'fives o-four'. Other coupons would add 'threes' or 'q's' for fraction, so the 5¼ per cent coupon would be 'five-q's' and 5¾ per cent coupon would be 'five-threes'.

GLOSSARY

A

Accreting: an instrument whose notional amount increases over its life, in accordance with a pre-set schedule or predefined index.

Accrued interest: The proportion of interest or coupon earned on an investment from the previous coupon payment date until the value date.

ACT/360: A day/year count convention taking the number of calendar days in a period and a 'year' of 360 days.

ACT/365: A day/year convention taking the number of calendar days in a period and a 'year' of 365 days. Under the International Swaps and Derivatives Association (ISDA) definitions used for interest rate swap documentation, ACT/365 means the same as ACT/ACT.

ACT/ACT: A day/year count convention taking the number of calendar days in a period and a 'year' equal to the number of days in the current coupon period multiplied by the coupon frequency. For an interest rate swap, that part of the interest period falling in a leap year is divided by 366 and the remainder is divided by 365.

All-in price: See **dirty price**.

Amortising: An amortising principal is one that decreases during the life of a deal, or is repaid in stages during a loan. Amortising an amount over a period of time also means accruing for it pro rata over the period. See also **accreting, bullet.**

Annuity: An investment providing a series of (generally equal) future cashflows.

Arbitrage: In theory a risk-free gain to exploit the same asset that is mispriced in a different market.

Ask: See **offer**.

Asset: Probable future economic benefit obtained or controlled as a result of past events or transactions. Generally classified as either current or long-term.

Asset and liability management (ALM): The practice of matching the term structure and cashflows of an organisation's asset and liability portfolios to maximise returns and minimise risk.

Asset-backed security: A security which is collateralised by specific assets

– such as mortgages – rather than by the intangible creditworthiness of the issuer.

Asset securitisation: The process whereby loans, receivables and other illiquid assets in the balance sheet are packaged into interest-bearing securities which offer attractive investment opportunities.

B

Balance sheet: Statement of the financial position of an enterprise at a specific point in time, giving assets, liabilities and stockholders' equity.

Base RPI: The starting level retail price index (inflation level) to which an index-linked security is linked.

Basis points (bps): In interest rate quotations, 0.01 per cent. So 1% = 100 basis points.

Basis risk: A form of market risk that arises whenever one kind of risk exposure is hedged with an instrument that behaves in a similar, but not necessarily identical, way. For instance a bank trading desk may use three-month interest rate futures to hedge its commercial paper or euronote programme. Although eurocurrency rates, to which futures prices respond, are well correlated with commercial paper rates, they do not always move in lock step. If therefore commercial paper rates move by 10 basis points but futures prices dropped by only 7 basis points, the 3 bp gap would be the basis risk.

Bearer bond: A bond for which physical possession of the certificate is proof of ownership. The issuer does not know the identity of the bond-holder. Traditionally the bond carries detachable coupons, one for each interest payment date, which are posted to the issuer when payment is due. At maturity the bond is redeemed by sending in the certificate for repayment. These days bearer bonds are usually settled electronically, and while no register of ownership is kept by the issuer, coupon payments may be made electronically.

Benchmark: A bond whose terms set a standard for the market. The benchmark usually has the greatest liquidity, the highest turnover and is usually the most frequently quoted. It also usually trades expensive to the yield curve, due to higher demand for it amongst institutional investors.

Beta: The sensitivity of a stock relative to swings in the overall market. The market has a beta of one, so a stock or portfolio with a beta greater than one will rise or fall more than the overall market, whereas a beta of less than one means that the stock is less volatile.

Bid: The price at which a market maker will buy bonds. A tight bid–offer spread is indicative of a liquid and competitive market. The bid rate in a repo is the interest rate at which the dealer will borrow the collateral and lend the cash. See also **offer**.

Bid–offer: The two-way price at which a market will buy and sell stock.

Bloomberg: The trading, analytics and news service produced by Bloomberg LP; also used to refer to the terminal itself.

Bond basis: An interest rate is quoted on a bond basis if it is on an ACT/365, ACT/ACT or 30/360 basis. In the short term (for accrued interest, for example), these three are different. Over a whole (non-leap) year, however they all equate to 1. In general, the expression 'bond basis' does not distinguish between them and is calculated as ACT/365. See also **money-market basis.**

Bond-equivalent yield: The yield that would be quoted on a US treasury bond that is trading at par and that has the same economic return and maturity as a given treasury bill.

Book-runner: See **lead underwriter**.

Bootstrapping: Building up successive zero-coupon yields from a combination of coupon-bearing yields.

Bpv: Basis point value. The price movement due to a one basis point change in yield.

Break-even inflation rate: The rate of inflation at which the return on a bond will match the return on an index linked security.

Breakeven principle: The idea that if I invest for one year, or for six months and then again for another six months, my return should be the same in each case because otherwise there would be an arbitrage (risk-free gain) possibility.

Broken date: A term for a loan that does not cover a standard period such as one month or six months. Also known as a 'cock-date'.

Broker-dealers: Members of the London Stock Exchange who may intermediate between customers and market makers; may also act as principals, transacting business with customers from their own holdings of stock.

Bulldog: Sterling domestic bonds issued by non-UK domiciled borrowers. These bonds trade under a similar arrangement to gilts and are settled via the Central Gilts Office (now CREST).

Bullet: A loan/deposit has a bullet maturity if the principal is all repaid at maturity. See also **amortising**.

C

Call: An option giving the holder the right, but not the obligation, to buy the option's underlying asset.

Call risk: The risk that a callable bond will be called.

Callable bond: A bond that provides the borrower with an option to redeem the issue before the original maturity date. In most cases certain terms are set before the issue, such as the date after which the bond is callable and the price at which the issuer may redeem the bond.

CEDEL: Centrale de Livraison de Valeurs Mobilières, a clearing system for euro-currency and international bonds, now known as *Clearstream*. It is located in Luxemburg and is jointly owned by a number of European banks.

Central Gilts Office (CGO): The office of the Bank of England which runs the computer-based settlement system for gilt-edged securities and certain other securities (mostly Bulldogs) for which the Bank acts as Registrar.

Clean price: The price of a bond excluding accrued coupon. The price quoted in the market for a bond is generally a clean price rather than a dirty price.

Compound interest: When some interest on an investment is paid before maturity and the investor can reinvest it to earn interest on interest, the interest is said to be compounded. Compounding generally assumes that the reinvestment rate is the same as the original rate. See also **simple interest**.

Continuous compounding: A mathematical, rather than practical, concept of compound interest where the period of compounding is infinitesimally small.

Contract date: The date on which a transaction is negotiated. See also **value date**.

Conventional gilts (included double-dated): Gilts on which interest payments and principal repayments are fixed.

Conversion factor: A number set by the trading exchange for all bonds that are deliverable into a bond futures contract. The conversion factor equalizes the coupon of the underlying bond to the notional coupon of the futures contract.

Coupon: The interest payment(s) made by the issuer of security to the holders, based on the coupon rate and the face value.

Cover: (a) the amount by which a bond is over-bid at auction; (b) to hedge an exposure arising from a transaction; (c) to arrange for delivery of a security that one has sold (shorted) but does not own.

Credit rating: The formal rating of credit quality assigned to a borrower by a rating agency such as Moody's or Standard & Poors.

Credit risk: The risk that a borrower defaults on a loan. Also risk of loss because of the deteriorating credit quality of an institution. For example, the credit risk of buying a bond issued by British Airways plc is the risk of British Airways being downgraded in credit rating or going into default.

Credit spread: The amount of interest over and above the government bond interest rate that a borrower must pay, to reflect its credit risk.

Credit watch: When a credit rating agency alerts the market that it is reviewing a borrower's credit rating.

Cum-dividend: The price of a bond including accrued interest.

Current yield: The simple yield of a bond, given by $(C/P) \times 100$ where C is the coupon and P is the dirty price.

D

Day count: The convention used to calculate accrued interest on bonds and interest on cash. For UK gilts the convention changed to ACT/ACT from ACT/365 on 1 November 1998. For cash the convention in sterling markets is ACT/365.

DBVs: An acronym for 'delivery by value', which refers to gilt collateral, and certain other sterling bond collateral, for use as security in a loan.

Debenture: In the US market, an unsecured domestic bond, backed by the general credit quality of the issuer. Debentures are issued under a trust deed or indenture. In the UK market, a bond that is secured against the general assets of the issuer.

Debt Management Office (DMO): An executive arm of the UK Treasury, responsible for cash management of the government's borrowing requirement. This includes responsibility for issuing government bonds (gilts), a function previously carried out by the Bank of England. The DMO began operations in April 1998.

Default: The event of non-payment of debt.

Default risk: See **credit risk**.

Derivative: Strictly, any financial instrument whose value is derived from another, such as a forward foreign exchange rate, a futures contract, an option or an interest rate swap. Forward deals to be settled in full are not always called derivatives, however.

Dirty price: The price of a bond after accrued interest has been added to the 'clean price'. The dirty price is the actual price paid in the market for the bond.

Discount factor: A number that is used to calculate present value, given by $1/(1+r)^n$ where r is the interest rate for n years.

Discount rate: The method of market quotation for certain securities (US and UK treasury bills, for example), expressing the return on the security as a proportion of the face value of the security received at maturity – as opposed to a yield which expresses the yield as a proportion of the original investment.

DMO: See **Debt Management Office**.

DMR: The Debt Management Report, published annually by HM Treasury.

Duration: A measure of the weighted average life of a bond or other series of cashflows, using the present values of the cashflows as the weights. See **modified duration**.

Duration gap: Measurement of the interest rate exposure of an institution.

Duration weighting: The process of using the modified duration value for bonds to calculate the exact nominal holdings in a spread position. This is necessary because £1 million nominal of a two-year bond is not equivalent to £1 million of, say, a five-year bond. The modified duration value of the five-year bond will be higher, indicating that its 'basis point value' (bpv) will be greater, and that therefore £1 million worth of this bond represents greater sensitivity to a move in interest rates (risk). As another example consider a fund manager holding £10 million of five-year bonds. The fund manager wishes to switch into a holding of two-year bonds with the same overall risk position. The basis point values of the bonds are 0.041583 and 0.022898 respectively. The ratio of the bpvs are 0.041583 / 0.022898 = 1.816. The fund manager therefore needs to switch into £10m × 1.816 = £18.160 million of the two-year bond.

E

ECU: European Currency Unit, a basket composed of European Union currencies, now defunct following the introduction of the eurocurrency.

Embedded option: An interest rate-sensitive option in debt instrument that affects its redemption. Such instruments include mortgage-backed securities and callable bonds.

Equity: The other name for shares. A share in ownership of a company.

Equity options: Options on shares of an individual common stock.

Euribor: The reference rate for the euro currency, set in Frankfurt.

Euro: The name for the domestic currency of the European Monetary Union. Not to be confused with eurocurrency.

Euroclear: An international clearing system for Eurocurrency and international securities. Euroclear is based in Brussels and managed by Morgan Guaranty Trust Company.

Eurocurrency: A currency owned by a non-resident of the country in which the currency is legal tender. Not to be confused with the euro.

Euro-issuance: The issue of gilts (or other securities) denominated in euros.

Euromarket: The international market in which eurocurrencies are traded.

Ex-dividend: The date after which a new holder of a bond is not entitled to the next coupon payment; alternatively the price of a bond minus the next coupon payment.

Ex-dividend (xd) date: A bond's record date for the payment of coupons. The coupon payment will be made to the person who is the registered holder of the stock on the xd date. For UK gilts this is seven working days before the coupon date.

Expected default rate: Estimate of the most likely rate of default of a counterparty expressed as a level of probability.

Extrapolation: The process of estimating a price or rate for value on a particular date by measuring past data and extending the trend line.

F

Face value: The principal amount of a security, generally repaid ('redeemed') all at maturity, but sometimes repaid in stages, on which the coupon amounts are calculated.

Fisher theory of interest: A theory of money and inflation developed by Irving Fisher in 1930, which demonstrated the relationship between money return and inflation.

Fixed price re-offer: The term meaning that once a Eurobond offer has been priced for initial sale in the primary market, that price will be supported by the syndicate for the rest of the day.

Fixing: See **LIBOR fixing**.

Floating rate: An interest rate set with reference to an external index. Also an instrument paying a floating rate is one where the rate of interest is refixed in line with market conditions at regular intervals such as every three or six months. In the current market, an exchange rate determined by market forces with no government intervention.

Floating rate gilt: Gilt issued with an interest rate adjusted periodically in line with market interbank rates.

Floating rate note: Capital market instrument on which the rate of interest payable is refixed in line with market conditions at regular intervals (usually six months).

FRA: Forward-rate agreement. A derivative contract that pays out the difference between a traded interested rate and what that rate is on expiry. Only the difference in interest is exchanged, there is no exchange of principal.

Fungible: A financial instrument that is equivalent in value to another, and easily exchanged or substituted. The best example is cash money, as a £10 note has the same value and is directly exchangeable with another £10 note. A bearer bond also has this quality.

Future: A futures contract is a contract to buy or sell securities or other goods at a future date at a pre-determined price. Futures contracts are usually standardised and traded on an exchange.

Future value: The amount of money achieved in the future, including interest, by investing a given amount of money now. See also **time value of money, present value**.

Futures contract: A deal to buy or sell some financial instrument or commodity for value on a future date. Unlike a forward deal, futures contracts are traded only on an exchange (rather than OTC), have standardised contract sizes and value dates, and are often only contracts for differences rather than deliverable.

G

G7: The 'Group of Seven' countries: the USA, Canada, the UK, Germany, France, Italy and Japan.

GEMM: A gilt-edged market maker, a bank or securities house registered with the Bank of England as a market maker in gilts. A GEMM is required to meet certain obligations as part of its function as a registered market maker, including making two-way price quotes at all times in all gilts and taking part in gilt auctions. The Debt Management Office now make a distinction between conventional gilt GEMMs and index-linked GEMMs, known as IG GEMMs.

General collateral (GC): Securities, which are not 'special', used as collateral against cash borrowing. A repo buyer will accept GC at any time that a specific stock is not quoted as required in the transaction. In the gilts market GC includes DBVs.

GIC: Guaranteed investment contract.

Gilt: A UK government sterling-denominated, listed security issued by HM Treasury with initial maturity of over 365 days when issued. The term 'gilt' (or gilt-edged) is a reference to the primary characteristic of gilts as an investment: their security.

Gilt-edged market maker: See GEMM.

GNP: Gross national product, the total monetary value of a country's output, as produced by citizens of that country.

Grey market: In the Eurobond market, that period between the marketing of a new bond and its actual first issue date.

Gross redemption yield (GRY): The same as yield to maturity; 'gross' because it does not take tax effects into account.

GRY: See **gross redemption yield.**

H

Hedge ratio: The ratio of the size of the position it is necessary to take in a particular instrument as a hedge against another, to the size of the position being hedged.

Hedging: Protecting against the risks arising from potential market movements in exchange rates, interest rates or other variables. See also **cover, arbitrage, speculation.**

I

IDB: Inter-dealer broker, in this context a broker that provide facilities for dealing in bonds between market makers.

IG: Index-linked gilt whose coupons and final redemption payment are related to the movements in the retail price index (RPI).

Immunisation: The process by which a bond portfolio is created that has an assured return for a specific time horizon irrespective of changes in interest rates. The mechanism underlying immunisation is a portfolio structure that balances the change in the value of a portfolio at the end of the investment horizon (time period) with the return gained from the reinvestment of cash flows from the portfolio. As such immunisation requires the portfolio manager to offset interest-rate risk and reinvestment risk.

Index-linked bonds: Securities whose coupon and/or maturity payment return is linked to an external reference such as the consumer prices index.

Inter-dealer broker: A firm that provides a broker service for market makers, with live anonymous prices being made available for trading.

Interest rate option: Option to pay or receive a specified rate of interest on or from a predetermined future date.

Interest-rate sensitivity: The sensitivity of a bond's price to changes in market interest rates. This sensitivity is measured by *modified duration*.

Interest rate swap: An agreement to exchange a series of cashflows determined in one currency, based on fixed or floating interest payments on an agreed notional principal, for a series of cashflows based in the same currency but on a different interest rate. May be combined with a currency swap.

Intermarket spread: A spread involving futures contracts in one market spread against futures contracts in another market.

Internal rate of return: The yield necessary to discount a series of cashflows to an NPV of zero.

Interpolation: The process of estimating a price or rate for value on a particular date by comparing the prices actually quoted for value dates either side. See also **extrapolation**.

Intervention: Purchases or sales of currencies in the market by central banks in an attempt to reduce exchange rate fluctuations or to maintain the value of a currency within a particular band, or at a particular level. Similarly, central bank operations in the money markets to maintain interest rates at a certain level.

ISMA: The International Securities Market Association. This association drew up with the PSA (now renamed the Bond Market Association) the PSA/ISMA Global Master Repurchase Agreement.

Issuer risk: Risk to an institution when it holds debt securities issued by another institution. See also **credit risk**.

Iteration: The repetitive mathematical process of estimating the answer to a problem, by trying how well this estimate fits the data, adjusting the estimate appropriately and trying against, until the fit is acceptably close. Used, for example, in calculating a bond's yield from its price.

J

Junk bonds: The common term for high yield bonds: higher risk, low-rated debt.

L

Lead manager: See **lead underwriter.**

Lead underwriter: The first-named bank in a syndicate.

LIBID: The London Interbank Bid Rate, the rate at which banks will pay for funds in the interbank market.

LIBOR: The London Interbank Offered Rate, the lending rate for all major currencies up to one-year set at 11am each day by the British Bankers Association.

LIBOR fixing: The LIBOR rate 'fixed' by the British Bankers Association (BBA) at 1100 hours each day, for maturities up to one year.

Lien: A security charge over an asset.

LIFFE: The London International Financial Futures and Options Exchange, the largest futures exchange in Europe.

Limean: The arithmetic average of LIBOR and LIBID rates.

Liquidation: Any transaction that closes out or offsets a futures or options position.

Liquidity: A word describing the ease with which one can undertake transactions in a particular market or instrument. A market where there are always ready buyers and sellers willing to transact at competitive prices is regarded as liquid. In banking, the term is also used to describe the requirement that a portion of a banks assets be held in short-term risk-free instruments, such as government bonds, T-bills and high-quality certificates of deposit.

Liquidity preference theory: A theory of the yield curve, saying that longer-dated interest rates should be higher than shorter-dated ones because they are less liquid.

Liquidity premium: The higher rate that should be paid on a longer-dated loan because it is less liquid than a shorter-dated loan.

Loan-equivalent amount: Description of derivative exposure which is used to compare the credit risk of derivatives with that of traditional bonds or bank loans.

Lognormal: A variable's probability distribution is lognormal if the logarithm of the variable has a normal distribution.

Lognormal distribution: The assumption that the log of today's interest rate, for example, minus the log of yesterday's rate is normally distributed.

Long: A surplus of purchases over sales of a given currency or asset, or a situation which naturally gives rise to an organisation benefiting from a strengthening of that currency or asset. To a money market dealer, however, a long position is a surplus of borrowings taken in over money lent out (which gives rise to a benefit if that currency weakens rather than strengthens). See also **short**.

LSE: London Stock Exchange.

M

Macaulay duration: See **duration**.

Market maker: Market participant who is committed, explicitly or otherwise, to quoting two-way bids and offering prices at all times in a particular market.

Market risk: Risks related to changes in prices of tradable macroeconomics variables, such as exchange rate risks.

Mark-to-market: The act of revaluing securities to current market values. Such revaluations should include both coupon accrued on the securities outstanding and interest accrued on the cash.

Modified duration: A measure of the proportional change in the price of a bond or other series of cashflows, relative to a change in yield. (Mathematically – / dirty price.) See also **duration**.

Money market: The market in cash deposits and loans of up to 12 months maturity.

Money market basis: The interest day-count for a money market instrument, which is generally ACT/360, or ACT/365 for sterling.

Money yield: The nominal return of a bond, without taking inflation effects into account.

Mortgage debenture: A bond that is backed by mortgage assets.

N

Name recognition: Credit risk of a borrower based on a perceived notion of the quality of its name, for example for a well-known company like Marks & Spencer plc, rather than as a result of any formal analysis.

Negative divergence: When at least two indicators, indexes or averages show conflicting or contradictory trends.

Net present value (NPV): The net present value of a series of cashflows is the sum of the present values of each cashflow (some or all of which may be negative).

Net redemption yield: The same as yield to maturity; 'net' because it takes tax effects into account.

O

O/N: See **overnight**.

Odd date: See **broken date**.

Offer: The price at which a market maker will sell bonds. Also called 'ask'.

Off-market: A rate that is not the current market rate.

Option: The right (but not the obligation) to buy or sell securities at a fixed price within a specified period.

OTC: Over the counter. Strictly speaking any transaction not conducted on a registered stock exchange. Trades conducted via the telephone between banks, and contracts such as FRAs and (non-exchange traded) options are said to be 'over-the-counter' instruments. OTC also refers to non-standard instruments or contracts traded between two parties: for example a client with a requirement for a specific risk to be hedged with a tailor-made instrument may enter into an OTC-structured option trade with a bank that makes markets in such products.

Over the counter: See **OTC**.

Overnight: The term for a loan of one-day maturity.

P

Paper: Another term for a bond or debt issue.

Par: In foreign exchange, when the outright and spot exchange rates are equal, the forward swap is zero or par. When the price of a security is equal to the face value, usually expressed as 100, it is said to be trading at par. A par swap rate is the current market rate for a fixed interest rate swap against LIBOR.

Par yield curve: A curve plotting maturity against yield for bonds priced at par.

Parallel shift: An upward or downward movement in the yield curve by the same magnitude along every point of the curve. For example, a 10 basis point upward parallel shift means that every point along the yield curve is shifted upwards by 10 basis points.

Plain vanilla: See **vanilla.**

Present value: The amount of money that needs to be invested now to achieve a given amount in the future when interest is added. See also **time value of money, future value**.

Price/earnings ratio: A ratio giving the price of a stock relative to the earnings per share.

Price factor: See **conversion factor**.

Primary market: The market for new debt, into which new bonds are issued. The primary market is made up of borrowers, investors and the investment banks that place new debt into the market, usually with their clients. Bonds that trade after they have been issued are said to be part of the secondary market.

Probability distribution: The mathematical description of how probable it is that the value of something is less than or equal to a particular level.

Probit procedures: Methods for analysing qualitative dependent methods where the dependent variable is binary, taking the values zero or one.

Put: A put option is an option to sell the commodity or instrument underlying the option. See also **call**.

R

Rate of recovery: Estimate of the percentage of the amount exposed to default – that is, the credit risk exposure – that is likely to be recovered by an institution if a counterparty defaults.

Real yield: the yield of a bond adjusted for the impact of inflation.

Record date: A coupon or other payment due on a security is paid by the issuer to whoever is registered on the record date as being the owner. See also **ex-dividend, cum-dividend**.

Redeem: A security is said to be redeemed when the principal is repaid.

Redemption yield: The rate of interest at which all future payments (coupons and redemption) on a bond are discounted so that their total equals the current price of the bond (inversely related to price).

Redenomination: A change in the currency unit in which the nominal value of a security is expressed (for example, from sterling to euro).

Register: Record of ownership of securities. For gilts, excluding bearer bonds, entry in an official register confers title.

Registered bond: A bond for which the issuer keeps a record (register) of its owners. Transfer of ownership must be notified and recorded in the register. Interest payments are posted (more usually electronically transferred) to the bondholder.

Registrar's Department: Department of the Bank of England which maintains the register of holdings of gilts.

Reinvestment risk: The risk that a bond coupon is reinvested at a lower interest-rate than was prevailing on bond issue.

Risk premium: A premium paid for taking on higher risk.

Running yield: Same as **current yield**.

Rump: A gilt issue so designated because it is illiquid, generally because there is a very small nominal amount left in existence.

S

S/N: See **spot/next**.

Secondary market: The market in instruments after they have been issued. Bonds are bought and sold after their initial issue by the borrower, and the marketplace for this buying and selling is referred to as the secondary market. The new issues market is the primary market.

Secured debt: Debt that is backed by collateral.

Securities and Exchange Commission: The central regulatory authority in the USA, responsible for policing the financial markets including the bond markets.

Securities lending: When a specific security is lent against some form of collateral. Also known as 'stock lending'.

Security: A financial asset sold initially for cash by a borrowing organisation (the 'issuer'). The security is often negotiable and usually has a maturity date when it is redeemed.

Sell/buy-back: Simultaneous spot sale and forward purchase of a security, with the forward price calculated to achieve an effect equivalent to a classic repo.

Settlement: The process of transferring stock from seller to buyer and arranging the corresponding movement of funds between the two parties.

Settlement bank: Bank which agrees to receive and make assured payments for gilts bought and sold by a CGO member.

Settlement date: Date on which transfer of gilts and payment occur, usually the next working date after the trade is conducted.

Settlement risk: The risk that occurs when there is a non-simultaneous exchange of value. Also known as 'delivery risk' and 'Herstatt risk'.

Sharpe ratio: A measure of the attractiveness of the return on an asset by comparing how much risk premium the investor can expect it to receive in return for the incremental risk (volatility) the investment carries. It is the ratio of the risk premium to the volatility of the asset.

Short: A short position is a surplus of sales over purchases of a given currency or asset, or a situation that naturally gives rise to an organisation benefiting from a weakening of that currency or asset. To a money market dealer, however, a short position is a surplus of money lent out over borrowings taken in (which give rise to a benefit if that currency strengthens rather than weakens). See also **long**.

Short date: A deal for value on a date other than spot but less than one month after spot.

Simple interest: When interest on an investment is paid all at maturity or not reinvested to earn interest on interest, the interest is said to be simple. See also **compound interest**.

Simple yield to maturity: Bond coupon plus principal gain/loss amortised over the time to maturity, as a proportion of the clean price per 100. Does not take time value of money into account. See **yield to maturity, current yield**.

Sinking fund: A cash reserve pool set up at the start of a bond issue by a borrower, and which is used to repay the bond in small increments each year.

Speculation: Putting on an exposure, whether long or short, in the belief that the assets being traded will rise or fall in price respectively.

Spot-next: An overnight loan that begins in two business days' time (known as 'spot' value).

Spot yield curve: The yield curve of spot (zero-coupon) interest rates.

Spread: The difference between the bid and offer prices in a quotation. Also a strategy involving the purchase of an instrument and the simultaneous sale of a similar related instrument, such as the purchase of a call option at one strike and the sale of a call option at a different strike.

Strip: A zero-coupon bond which is produced by separating a standard coupon-bearing bond into its constituent principal and interest components. To strip a bond is to separate its principal amount and its coupons and trade each individual cash flow as a separate instrument ('*s*eparately *t*raded and *r*egistered for *i*nterest and *p*rincipal'). Also, a strip of futures is a series of short-term futures contracts with consecutive delivery dates, which together create the effect of a longer term instrument (for example, four consecutive three-month futures contracts as a hedge against a one-year swap). A strip of FRAs is similar.

Switch: Exchanges of one gilt holding for another, sometimes entered into between the DMO and a GEMM as part of the DMO's secondary market operations.

Syndicate: A group of banks involved in a bond or loan deal with one borrower.

T

Tail: In a bond auction, the difference between the highest yield bid for a bond and the average yield of all the received bids.

Term: The time between the beginning and end of a deal or investment.

Time value of money: The concept that a future cashflow can be valued as the amount of money which it is necessary to invest now in order to achieve that cashflow in the future. See also **present value, future value**.

TIPS: The name for US Treasury index-linked securities.

Today/tomorrow: See **overnight**.

Tom/next: A transaction from the next working day ('tomorrow') until the day after ('next day – that is, spot in the foreign exchange market).

Tranche: One of a series of two or more issues with the same coupon rate and maturity date. The tranches become fungible at a future date, usually just after the first coupon date.

Transaction risk: Extent to which the value of transactions that have already been agreed is affected by market risk.

Transparent: A term used to refer to how clear asset prices are in a market. A transparent market is one in which a majority of market participants are aware of what level a particular bond or instrument is trading.

U

Uncovered option: When the writer of the option does not own the underlying security. Also known as a 'naked option'.

Undated gilts: Gilts for which there is no final date by which the gilt must be redeemed.

Underlying: The underlying of a futures or option contract is the commodity of financial instrument on which the contract depends. Thus the underlying for a bond option is the bond; the underlying for a short-term interest rate futures contract is typically a three-month deposit.

Underwriting: An arrangement by which a company is guaranteed that an issue of debt (bonds) will raise a given amount of cash. Underwriting is carried out by investment banks, which undertake to purchase any part of the debt issue not taken up by the public. A commission is charged for this service.

Unsecured debt: A loan that is not backed by any collateral being put up by the borrower.

V

Value date: The date on which a deal is to be consummated. In some bond markets, the value date for coupon accruals can sometimes differ from the settlement date.

Vanilla: A vanilla transaction is a straightforward one.

W

Warrant: A security giving the holder a right to subscribe to a share or bond at a given price and from a certain date. If this right is not exercised before the maturity date, the warrant will expire worthless.

Write: To sell an option is to write it. The person selling an option is known as 'the writer'.

Writer: The same as 'seller' of an option.

Y

Yield: The interest rate that can be earned on an investment, currently quoted by the market or implied by the current market price for the investment – as opposed to the coupon paid by an issuer on a security, which is based on the coupon rate and the face value. For a bond, generally the same as yield to maturity unless otherwise specified.

Yield curve: Graphical representation of the maturity structure of interest rates, plotting yields of bonds that are all of the same class or credit quality against the maturity of the bonds.

Yield to maturity: The internal rate of return of a bond, the rate used to discount the cashflows of a bond in order to obtain the price.

YTM: See **yield to maturity**.

Z

Zero-premium option: Generic term for options for which there is no premium, either because the buyer undertakes to forgo a percentage of any gain or because he or she offsets the cost by writing other options.

Zero-coupon: A zero-coupon security is one that does not pay a coupon. Its price is correspondingly less to compensate for this. A zero-coupon yield is the yield that a zero-coupon investment for that term would have if it were consistent with the par yield curve.

Zero-coupon bond: Bond on which no coupon is paid. It is either issued at a discount or redeemed at a premium to face value.

Zero-coupon swap: Swap converting the payment pattern of a zero-coupon bond, either to that of a normal, coupon-paying fixed-rate bond or to a floating rate.

FURTHER READING

There are lots of books out there on the markets, on investing, on bonds, and on finance generally. As a private investor you only need to read a few of them. Keep in touch on a more frequent basis by occasionally checking out the *Financial Times* and *Investors Chronicle*, but you don't need to read them every day or week.

Be wary of 'get rich quick' books or books that purport to tell you the 'inside secrets' and so on. Stick to the fundamentals, as Bud Fox's colleague said in *Wall Street*, and you should be OK.

The books below all have some value for private investors. The Peter Temple book is excellent; the Crescenzi and Faerber books concentrate only on the US viewpoint. All are worth reading. Andrew Leach's book has much useful information, such as a list of private client stockbrokers and their contact details.

My own book *Fixed Income Markets* is a bit heavy going for the beginner, but at least you know you've arrived when you start reading it!

Happy reading!

BOOK LIST

Choudhry, M., *Bond Market Securities*, FT Prentice Hall 2001.

Choudhry, M., *The Gilt-Edged Market*, Butterworth-Heinemann 2003.

Choudhry, M., *Fixed Income Markets*, John Wiley 2005.

Crescenzi, A., *The Strategic Bond Investor*, McGraw Hill, 2002.

Faerber, E., *All About Bonds and Bond Mutual Funds*, McGraw Hill, 2000.

Gough, L., *How the Stock Market Really Works*, FT Prentice Hall, 2001.

Leach, A., *Complete Guide to Investment*, Random House, 2001.

Temple, P., *First Steps In Bonds*, FT Prentice Hall, 2002.

Thomsett, M., *Getting Started In Bonds*, John Wiley, 2001.

Useful websites

Originator	Website	Type
ADVFN	www.advfn.com	Portal
APCIMS	www.apcims.co.uk	Trade association
Bank of England	www.bankofengland.co.uk	Central bank
Barclays Capital	www.barclayscapital.com	Investment banks
Bloomberg	www.bloomberg.com www.bloomberg.co.uk	News service
Bond Resources	www.bondresources.com	General knowledge
Calculator Web	www.calculatorweb.com	Yield calculator
Bonds Online	www.bondsonline.com	Yield calculator
UK Debt Management Office	www.dmo.gov.uk	Gilt issuance office
Economist	www.economist.com	News magazine
European Central Bank	www.ecb.int	Central bank
US Federal Reserve	www.federalreserve.gov	Central bank
Finance Center	www.financecenter.com	Yield calculator
Financial Times	www.ft.com	Newspaper
FT Market Watch	www.ftmarketwatch.com	Price listing
FT Your Money	www.ftyourmoney.com	UK personal finance
HM Treasury	www.hm-treasury.gov.uk	UK Treasury
Interactive Investor	www.iii.com	Web portal
Investing in Bonds	www.investinginbonds.com	General knowledge
Investors Chronicle	www.investorschronicle.co.uk	News magazine

JPMorgan Chase Bank	www.jpmorgan.com	Investment bank
Kauders Portfolio Management	www.gilt.co.uk	Fund management adviser
LIFFE	www.liffe.com	Futures exchange
London Stock Exchange	www.londonstockexchange.com	Stock exchange
Lombard Street Research	www.lombard-st.co.uk	Research and economics
Long Bond	www.longbond.com	General knowledge
Merrill Lynch	www.mlim.co.uk	Fund manager
Moody's	www.moodys.com	Ratings agency
ONS	www.statistics.gov.uk	National statistics
PIMCO	www.pimco.com	Commentary
Quote.com	www.quote.com	Price service
Reuters	http://quotes.reuters.com	News service
Nat West	www.rbs.co.uk	Unit trust manager
Wall Street Journal	www.wsj.com	Newspaper
YieldCurve.com	www.yieldcurve.com	Fixed income research